D1383560

DR. PHIL
Self-Help Guru and TV Superstar

Other titles in the **People to Know Today** series:

Lance Armstrong
Cycling, Surviving, Inspiring Hope
ISBN-13: 978-0-7660-2694-0
ISBN-10:   0-7660-2694-9

Bill Gates
Computer Mogul and Philanthropist
ISBN-13: 978-0-7660-2693-3
ISBN-10:   0-7660-2693-0

George W. Bush
President in a Turbulent World
ISBN-13: 978-0-7660-2628-5
ISBN-10:   0-7660-2628-0

Dorothea Lange
A Life in Pictures
ISBN-13: 978-0-7660-2697-1
ISBN-10:   0-7660-2697-3

Laura Bush
Portrait of a First Lady
ISBN-13: 978-0-7660-2629-2
ISBN-10:   0-7660-2629-9

J. K. Rowling
Author of *Harry Potter*
ISBN-13: 978-0-7660-1850-1
ISBN-10:   0-7660-1850-4

Walt Disney
Genius of Entertainment
ISBN-13: 978-0-7660-2624-7
ISBN-10:   0-7660-2624-8

Arnold Schwarzenegger
From Superstar to Governor
ISBN-13: 978-0-7660-2625-4
ISBN-10:   0-7660-2625-6

Robert Frost
The Life of America's Poet
ISBN-13: 978-0-7660-2627-8
ISBN-10:   0-7660-2627-2

Sam Walton
Business Genius of Wal-Mart
ISBN-13: 978-0-7660-2692-6
ISBN-10:   0-7660-2692-2

People to Know Today

DR. PHIL
Self-Help Guru and TV Superstar

By Mary Main

Enslow Publishers, Inc.
40 Industrial Road
Box 398
Berkeley Heights, NJ 07922
USA

http://www.enslow.com

Dedication
For Anne and Mitch Disney, who live Family First every day.

Acknowledgments
Thank you to Ellen Herscher for her everlasting generosity and support, and for being the sister I always wanted.

Library of Congress Cataloging-in-Publication Data

Main, Mary.
    Dr. Phil : self-help guru and TV superstar / by Mary Main.
        p. cm. — (People to know today)
    Includes bibliographical references and index.
    ISBN-13: 978-0-7660-2696-4
    ISBN-10: 0-7660-2696-5
    1. McGraw, Phillip C., 1950–. 2. Psychologists—United States—Biography—Juvenile literature.
3. Television personalities—United States—Biography—Juvenile literature. I. Title. II. Title:
Doctor Phil.
BF109.M365M35 2007
150.92—dc22
[B]

                          2006034070

Printed in the United States of America

10 9 8 7 6 5 4 3 2 1

To Our Readers: We have done our best to make sure all Internet addresses in this book were active and appropriate when we went to press. However, the author and publisher have no control over and assume no liability for the material available on those Internet sites or on other Web sites they may link to. Any comments or suggestions can be sent by e-mail to comments@enslow.com or to the address on the back cover.

Photos and Illustration: AP/Wide World Photos, pp. 3, 6, 10, 35, 39, 72, 74, 77, 85, 95, 102, 103; David Woo, Dallas Morning News, pp. 50, 55, 65; Everett Collection, Inc., pp. 50, 55, 58, 66, 83, 104; Shawnee Mission North High School, pp. 15, 24, 28, 30.

Cover Illustration: Everett Collection, Inc.

CONTENTS

1. Midnight Meeting 7

2. Country Boy 13

3. Taking Flight 22

4. Like Father, Like Son 33

5. Becoming Doctor McGraw 43

6. Courtroom Wizard 53

7. Counselor and Life Strategist 62

8. Family Fame 70

9. Television Guru 81

10. Giving Back 89

11. Family First 99

Chronology 106

Chapter Notes 110

Books by Dr. Phil McGraw 122

Further Reading 123

Internet Addresses 124

Index 125

Dr. Phil McGraw

1
MIDNIGHT MEETING

Dr. Phil McGraw could not sleep. It was late at night in a rambling three-story house that doubled as an inn just outside Amarillo, Texas. A cold wind from the north moaned and creaked around the house that winter night in 1998. Outside, armed guards kept watch for intruders. McGraw believed that he and the other guests in the inn could be in danger. They had even received death threats.[1] Still, McGraw believed that renting all nine rooms in the house in the heart of cattle country was safer than staying in a hotel. Here, security guards could keep watch twenty-four hours a day. In the basement game room, McGraw worked late into the night.

It was well after midnight when McGraw heard a tap on his door. He crossed the room and opened the door. One of the most famous women in the world stood on the doorstep looking tired and worried. Dressed in flannel pajamas and fuzzy slippers, Oprah Winfrey looked younger than her years. She had tears in her eyes.[2]

McGraw knew why Winfrey was upset. Things were not going well for the queen of daytime television. Winfrey had been sued by the Texas Cattlemen for millions of dollars. Oprah had vowed on her television show that she would never eat another hamburger. A guest on the show had advised her that American cattle were fed ground-up beef from cows with Mad Cow Disease. He convinced Oprah that beef was toxic. The cattlemen claimed her criticism of hamburger resulted in reduced profits for the beef business.

The court had forced her to come for the trial to the heart of cattle country, where she rented all nine rooms of the inn for her legal team. If Winfrey lost this lawsuit, she would not only lose millions of dollars. McGraw believed there would be an even more serious consequence. He believed Oprah would become a target for many other lawsuits.

Self-pity was not part of Winfrey's personality, but she did feel frustrated and confused. "Why is this happening to *me*?" she asked McGraw.[3] She could not believe the Texas cattlemen blamed her for their business losses. She thought of herself as a nice person. She had always tried to do good in the world and believed the hostility directed at her was totally unfair. Buttons were even being passed out in town with a red line drawn through her face. McGraw understood just how she felt.[4]

An experienced psychotherapist, McGraw had left his therapy practice seven years earlier to form a trial consulting firm called Courtroom Sciences, Inc. (CSI) with a partner. His job was to advise lawyers how to win at trial. Winfrey's lawyer had hired McGraw and CSI to make sure she won her jury trial against the cattlemen. But the way things were going, it looked like Winfrey was in trouble because of her attitude. She was coming across as hostile and suspicious in the courtroom. McGraw believed if things continued in this way, Winfrey would lose her case to the cattlemen.[5]

It was McGraw's job to turn the trial around for Oprah Winfrey.

McGraw had come a long way from the unhappiness and poverty he experienced as a young boy. His family had once been so poor they ate mustard and ketchup sandwiches for dinner. He had decided his life would be different. He pursued his education and became a successful therapist and trial consultant. At this moment, one of the most famous women in the world looked to him for advice.

It was McGraw's job to turn the trial around for Oprah Winfrey. He had grown fond of her as a friend, but he squelched his desire to tell her not to worry.

He knew better. He knew she should be worried. Eventually Winfrey would take the witness stand to tell her story. McGraw knew if she did not stop dwelling on why the lawsuit had happened to her and start acting like the confident woman she had once been, the jury might very well decide against her.

Every day, Oprah's lawyer Chip Babcock kept asking McGraw, "Is she ready? We must get her ready."[6] Looking at her late that night, McGraw knew she was not ready.

McGraw and Winfrey sat across from each other in the game room. Taking her hand, he looked her in

Oprah Winfrey celebrates outside the courthouse in Amarillo, Texas, after a jury ruled in her favor on February 26, 1998. Winfrey had been sued by an association of Texas cattlemen for allegedly defaming the beef industry on one of her programs.

the eye and said firmly, "You'd better wake up, girl, and wake up *now*. It *is* really happening. You'd better *get over it* and get in the game, or these good ol' boys are going to hand you your [butt] on a platter."[7]

At first Winfrey looked shocked at McGraw's blunt words. But as the words sank in, she knew he was right. In fact, McGraw's plea to get real had revived her real self. His ability to analyze a problem and help her understand how to solve the problem impressed her. Here was a guy who could cut to the chase. She looked McGraw in the eye and replied, "No they will not."[8]

McGraw smiled at her fighting words. He believed at that very moment the cattlemen lost their case.[9] And he was right. At the end of the six-week trial, the jury announced that Oprah Winfrey had done nothing wrong. The cattlemen got no money at all. And Oprah Winfrey said that McGraw "gave myself back to me."[10]

What is a Lawsuit?

When a person believes a wrong has been committed against him, he may hire an attorney and file a lawsuit. The attorney files papers, called *pleadings*, with the court. The first of these pleadings is called the *Complaint*. The Complaint states the basic facts of the case; names everyone involved in the case; states legal theory to back up the claim; and states the outcome demanded by the lawsuit, usually money. The person who files the lawsuit is called the *Plaintiff*. The person being sued is called the *Defendant*. The lawyers will argue the case in court, and a judge or jury will decide whether the Plaintiff wins or loses.

Winfrey knew that McGraw's sharp psychological insights and his old-fashioned common sense were a winning combination. She realized he could help other people as he had helped her. Not long after their victory in court, McGraw was invited to make his first guest appearance on *The Oprah Winfrey Show.*

2
COUNTRY
BOY

Phillip Calvin McGraw was born on September 1, 1950, in Vinita, Oklahoma. His father, Joe McGraw, was the new football coach at Vinita High School. His mother, Jerry McGraw, was a stay-at-home wife and mother.

Anticipation filled the air on the first evening in September, on the opening night of the football season in Vinita. Oklahomans have always been avid sports fans, and the high school football games drew a lot of fanfare. Coach McGraw, fresh out of college himself, could hardly wait to try out his coaching skills in the season opener.[1] But an hour before kickoff that night, Jerry went into labor.

The small local hospital contained only eighteen beds. Joe McGraw paced outside the delivery room wondering if he would make the game that night. Fifteen minutes before kickoff time, Jerry gave birth to a baby boy. Coach McGraw was forced to miss his first game. It did not matter. He and his wife Jerry were thrilled that their third-born child was a boy.[2] Soon, they would take little Phil home to join his two sisters, Donna and Deana.

Dr. Phil, as he is known today, had humble beginnings. The hospital maternity ward consisted of only four beds, and carefully-wrapped babies were often placed in dresser drawers to sleep.[3] When Baby Phil left the hospital, he was taken to his family's tiny wood house in a neighborhood near the railroad tracks. This home on South Scraper Street is still there today near the Vinita Flag and Apron Company.

Phil's parents, Joe and Jerry, grew up in hard-working families in the small town of Munday, Texas. Munday had a population of 1,500 people and was located in Knox County in northwest central Texas, halfway between Wichita Falls and Abilene. This part of Texas was sparsely populated and consisted of rolling plains covered with spiny mesquite.

The soil was good for farming and raising cattle, and Munday's residents worked at both industries. In the 1930s, the era of the Great Depression, cotton crops provided most people with their livelihoods. As youngsters, both Joe and Jerry worked in the fields chopping cotton. Cotton crops were so important to the town that schools let out for two weeks during the harvest so young people could work. It was hard to make a living. Many people struggled to survive.

Joe McGraw was named after his father, a butcher in a grocery store in town. His three younger siblings were triplets. In some ways, Joe's childhood was not a

Phil McGraw helps tackle an opposing player during a high school football game. Football was a big part of the McGraw family life.

happy one. He was beaten and abused by his mother all through his childhood.[4] Outside the home, Joe lived the life of a country boy, riding donkeys with his friends and playing hockey with sticks and a tin can in vacant lots. He got good grades in school and liked to read books and newspapers.[5]

Like Joe, Jerry grew up in a family that was uneducated and hard-working. Somewhat shy, Jerry loved the country. She continued to be a gardener throughout her life.

At Munday High School, Joe and Jerry dated steadily. Joe was big and athletic, standing just over six feet and weighing nearly 200 pounds. He played basketball and football and ran track. As the football team's running back and star, he led his team to a district championship in his senior year.[6]

Joe and Jerry decided to get married before Joe shipped out with the Navy during World War II. After Joe completed his Navy service and returned to Texas, he decided to enter college on the GI Bill. No one in the family had ever gone to college, and Joe's family mocked him for his choice. Family members accused him of "playing student" and wasting his life in a book instead of getting a real job.[7] But Joe believed a college education would help him and Jerry have a better life. He ignored the family's critical remarks. The young couple left for Oklahoma, where the University of Tulsa offered Joe a scholarship to play football.

Joe graduated from the University of Tulsa with mediocre grades. However, he received a degree in education and in 1950 landed the coaching and teaching job in Vinita. Jerry worked at home keeping house and taking care of the children.

Located on Route 66 in the northeastern corner of Oklahoma, Vinita was a lively little town with a cowboy flavor. Dime stores, dress shops, shoe stores, small cafés, and three movie theaters made up the town center. People congregated on Main Street, especially on Saturdays, when the farmers arrived to do their trading. Trains often rumbled over the tracks, letting out whistle blasts and blocking local traffic. Today, Vinita is famous for having the largest McDonald's restaurant in the world.[8]

As the local football coach, Joe McGraw was a celebrity in town, but that did not mean he earned a lot of money. His duties—coaching football and track, teaching marriage and family classes, and acting as a school guidance counselor—earned him a modest salary. Joe was cheerful and friendly with the students but could be tough at times, especially on the football field.[9] In spite of Joe's coaching, the football teams lost more games than they won.

When Phil was two years old, Joe decided to quit his job at Vinita High School and go to work in the oil industry. His new job as a salesman involved moving his family back and forth between towns in Oklahoma,

Kansas, Texas, and Colorado. As children, Phil and his older sisters Donna and Deana and his younger sister Brenda did not have one secure home base.

Being the only boy, Phil got lots of attention from his mother and sisters. When he was three years old, his sisters took him with them to school. He even carried a sack lunch like Donna and Deana. According to his mother, the girls idolized little Phil. But being the only boy in the family brought heavy responsibility. In Texas, boys were expected to work hard and take care of the girls in the family. Phil spent more of his childhood working than playing.[10]

Phil spent summers in Munday, Texas, with his maternal grandparents, Mabel and Cal Stevens. Mabel, called Nanny by the family, was a tiny woman under five feet tall. Cal towered over her at almost seven feet tall. Mabel and Cal were smart, hardworking country folks. Mabel took in ironing to make money and picked plums for her homemade jelly. She was also known to dip snuff, a moist, finely-ground chewing tobacco. Sometimes the tobacco dribbled down her chin.[11]

Cal, owner of the local freight warehouse in Munday, drove his truck so slowly that kids would run alongside for fun. The townspeople said Cal never had to replace his truck tires because he drove so slow they never wore out.[12]

Mabel and Cal had an unusual relationship for a married couple. They did not do the so-called normal things believed to make a good marriage, yet they got alone fine. They spoke very few words to each other, but they obviously loved each other. Phil was fascinated by his grandparents and spent a lot of time trying to figure out what made them tick.[13]

Phil was eight years old when he met a man who became an instant hero to him. Gene Knight was a pilot who delivered cases of whiskey throughout the state of Oklahoma. One Saturday, Phil's father took him out to a cotton patch in the country to see Knight's plane come in for a landing. When Knight stepped out of his airplane, Phil thought he looked like a movie star, with his black hair and leather flying jacket. Knight was about six feet four inches tall and had a big grin on his face. Phil knew instantly Knight was someone who passionately enjoyed what he did for a living.[14]

Finally, the day came when Knight invited Phil to go for an airplane ride with him. Years later, Dr. Phil McGraw would write: "Buck Rogers had nothing on me! As soon as we were airborne, I told myself, I'm gonna be a pilot, and just as soon as I came of age, I got my license. I have been flying my entire life, a direct result of Gene Knight's influence."[15]

As a boy, Phil worked

"As soon as we were airborne, I told myself, I'm gonna be a pilot, and just as soon as I came of age, I got my license."

Getting a Pilot's License

Flying an airplane is not a hard skill to learn. All kinds of people have experienced the thrill of taking the controls and soaring above the earth. Rules for earning a pilot's license are enforced by the Federal Aviation Administration (FAA). Lessons may begin at age 16, but a student must be 17 years old to get a license. Students must log at least 40 hours of flight. Out of that, 20 hours must be spent with an instructor and 10 hours spent in solo flight. The average student logs 65 hours. Students must perform certain maneuvers before they can fly solo, including safe takeoffs and landings. A medical certificate and a student pilot's certificate are required in order to fly solo.[17] Flying is safer than most forms of transportation and can become an exciting part of anyone's life.

hard to contribute to the family's livelihood. The family lived on the edge of poverty and scrapped for everything they got. Phil mowed lawns, delivered newspapers, and helped his father in his sales job. Even as a small boy, he was forced to take on the duties of manhood and had little time to relax and play like other kids.[16]

When Phil was in fifth grade, his family lived in a small tract house outside Denver, Colorado. All the houses were the same, with three bedrooms, one bath, and a single-car garage. Fifth grade was going well for Phil. He had plenty of friends, got good grades, and won the Athlete of the Year award. His favorite teacher, Mrs. Johnson, was in charge of his homeroom.

One day at recess, a gang of bullies from the sixth grade started picking on a bunch of younger kids, including Phil and his buddies. The bullies threw one of Phil's friends to the ground. They began pushing and shoving Phil and his friends. Phil threw a basketball as hard as he could and hit one of the bullies in the face. Then he hauled off and socked one of them. A huge fight broke out on the playground.

Phil and the other boys were herded into the principal's office. Mrs. Johnson was called. Phil stood there in his ripped shirt with his nose bleeding, chunks of gravel embedded in his cheek, and a huge knot on his forehead. He felt like everything would be all right as soon as Mrs. Johnson arrived. He would explain to her how the bullies had started the fight. It did not turn out that way. Mrs. Johnson walked in, looked at Phil, and started yelling at him. She never even asked him what happened.

Many years later, he would call this experience one of the defining moments in his life. "In a flash, it hit me right there in that principal's office that I could no longer assume that life was fair. It was not fair."[18] After that, Phil decided he could not depend on people in authority to take care of him. Although he was proud of the fact he had defended his friends, he felt betrayed by Mrs. Johnson. He realized he had the ability and the duty to take care of himself. From then on, he worked toward becoming strong and self-reliant.

3

TAKING FLIGHT

In 1962, when Phil was twelve years old, his dream of flying an airplane came true. His father, Joe McGraw, worked at a job delivering drill bits and tools to the oil fields. Phil often went along on these trips. Joe taught Phil to fly and allowed his son to take the controls when they made deliveries.

Phil's flying trips with his father over the Rocky Mountains could be hair-raising experiences. Phil and Joe often flew at two in the morning and landed on mountain landing strips, loading and unloading the plane in the dead of night. The wind blew so hard before they took off that men would grab tight to the wings of the McGraws' plane and guide it into the wind on the runway so it would not blow over.[1] Father and son worked well together.

But at home, Phil felt cut off from his father, mother, and three sisters. The family's tiny, paint-peeled tract house near Denver, Colorado, depressed him. His father had become a severe and chronic alcoholic. Phil and his dad clashed violently.[2] Although Jerry was affectionate with her children, she and Joe fought constantly. Joe tried to pressure Jerry into being more social with his business associates. She refused, saying she hated to entertain.[3]

Phil's two older sisters eloped as teenagers and moved away. When they came back home, they seemed different to Phil. He could not talk to them like he used to. Phil tried to comfort his younger sister Brenda, but she was an anxious child who was afraid to leave home.[4]

Since Phil was the only boy in the family, he had his own tiny bedroom and spent most of his time alone in his room without a television or even a radio. He came and went through his bedroom window. He felt like he lived in two worlds, the world at home and the world of friends and school.[5]

At night, Phil climbed out his bedroom window and roamed the streets. He got very little sleep because his fifty-mile paper route with his father began at 4:30 A.M. and lasted for two and a half hours.[6] After delivering papers with Joe, Phil entered the world of friends, school, and sports. Class work did not excite him, but he still pulled A+ grades on tests, and his teachers liked him.

In sports, Phil felt the best about himself. A strong, coordinated boy, he could master any sport he played. He felt embarrassed that his family was so poor compared to the other kids, but on the playing field he was just like everybody else. His buddies admired him for his athletic ability, and he enjoyed belonging to a group of friends.[7]

At times, Phil hated his father. Joe smoked big cigars, and Phil thought they made him stink.[8] Phil lived in constant fear that Joe would embarrass the

Phil McGraw dozes off in class. His extra-curricular activities and jobs left him little time to rest.

family with his drunkenness. And Joe often bought things he could not afford and put the family in debt.[9] On the other hand, Phil learned a strong work ethic from his father. Joe advised Phil never to be scared by any person or challenge.[10] Joe's job changes and family moves forced Phil to adapt to different places. His dad had many sayings that taught Phil the basic truths of life. One of Joe's favorite sayings was "Create your own experience. Make a decision and pull the trigger."[11] Although it was hard on his wife and children, Joe McGraw did just that in his own life. This taught Phil that a person could decide to change his or her life and put those changes into action.

His dad also said "worrying is like rocking in a chair: it's something to do, but you don't get any- where."[12] In other words, if something is not going right in your life, instead of worrying about it, do something about it. From his dad, Phil learned to make a plan and follow through on that plan.

Phil and his friends often met in a field behind his house. The field held a big trench they called the "Valley of Death." The trench was four feet deep and ran from one end of the lot to the other. Using a single two-by-six board, the boys built a narrow bridge across the trench. They rode their bikes over this board at full speed. Phil found that when he focused on racing smoothly to the other end of the board, he would make it to the other side. If he rode up to the board fearing he might slip off, he would usually fall. Racing over the "Valley of Death" taught Phil to focus on his goal and shut out all obstacles.[13]

In 1964, when Phil was fourteen years old, Joe McGraw decided to pull the trigger yet again and leave his job in sales to return to college. At the age of forty, Joe wanted to earn his Ph.D. in psychology from the University of Oklahoma. The family's income dropped drastically after Joe quit his job. Jerry took a job at Sears and worked long hours to put food on the table. Still, sometimes the only dinner the McGraws could afford was ketchup-and-mustard sandwiches. The family's poverty was a wake-up call for Phil. He realized if they did not work, they did not eat. Phil saw that the way he lived his life would bring certain kinds of results. He wanted those results to be good ones.[14]

> **Racing over the "Valley of Death" taught Phil to focus on his goal and shut out all obstacles.**

One day Phil's junior high school football team took on the local Salvation Army team. Phil's team had tough-looking, black uniforms and thought they would annihilate the Salvation Army boys, who looked silly in their rolled up jeans and loafers. It did not turn out that way. The Salvation Army kids slaughtered Phil's team. Phil was shocked. "At that point I really got interested in why some people, with all the advantages in the world, don't do well, and those with no advantages can be absolute champions."[15]

During the time Joe went to grad school, the McGraws moved in with Phil's oldest sister, Deana, and her husband in Oklahoma City. Phil was a big boy with a big appetite. He loved chili cheese dogs, and he could eat three of the foot-long sandwiches in one sitting.

Despite the family's struggle to make ends meet, Phil's father arranged to buy him a Yamaha 250 motorcycle. There were only two rules: First, Phil must ride inside their neighborhood. Second, his friends must never ride the motorcycle, because Joe could not afford insurance. Three weeks later, Phil broke his dad's rule and let a buddy ride his bike.

His friend screamed down the street and hit a Buick. Phil heard the crash and got a sick feeling in the pit of his stomach. His friend was thrown 300 feet in the air. He landed on his stomach, smashed his face into the curb, and almost killed himself. The Yamaha was totaled.

Joe showed up at the hospital where Phil was visiting his injured friend. He told Phil, "Son, I hope and pray that he took that motorcycle without your permission, or you're in a lot of trouble and our family is in a lot of trouble." Phil was scared to death to tell his dad he had gone against his orders. He considered lying—telling his dad his buddy took the bike without permission. In the end, he decided not to lie no matter what the cost. He admitted to his dad that he had let his buddy ride the bike.

He knew he was about to receive some dire punishment. His dad thought for a long time. Finally, he said, "Well, son, we will just have to work it out." Phil was blown away by how his dad chose to support him in the situation. Phil telling Joe the truth when it would have been so much easier to lie was worth more to his father than any amount of money.[16]

Joe decided to take Phil with him to Kansas while pursuing his internship in psychology. The rest of the family stayed behind in Oklahoma. Phil attended Shawnee Mission North High School, a suburban school in a red brick building in Kansas City. At

A photo of Phil McGraw (circled) and some his fellow members of the Shawnee Mission North High School football team from his high school yearbook.

Shawnee, most of the kids came from families that earned good incomes and lived in nice houses. Phil was embarrassed to be the guy who lived in an apartment with no nice clothes, no car, and no money. Eventually, Phil and Joe moved into a split level house. His father was rarely home to supervise him. Phil spent a lot of time alone and missed his mother and sisters.[17]

At the age of sixteen, Phil stood six feet four inches tall and had a receding hairline. He looked older than the other kids at school and got noticed when he walked down the halls. He earned a spot on the Shawnee football team. Once again, athletics gave him a purpose in life. At times, his love for sports was the only thing that kept him from dropping out of high school.[18] Phil was a tough lineman on the gridiron. Even two broken thumbs set in casts could not stop him from plowing into opposing teams.[19]

As a jock, Phil earned the respect of his peers. Eventually, his father bought him a used car. Phil worked at the Hallmark card plant at night so he could afford to fix his car and go on dates.

Phil dated Debbie Higgins, the most popular girl in school. Higgins, the head cheerleader, was a vivacious brown-eyed girl who was friendly to everyone, not just the cool kids. Debbie won every election she entered, including homecoming queen. Phil and Debbie were together so much that some of their teachers called them "Mr. and Mrs. McGraw."

Once in a while, Debbie and Phil would argue and break up for a while. None of the other guys dared to ask Debbie out during those times. They knew they would have to face an angry Phil if they did.[20]

Phil did not enjoy his classes, but he wanted to attend college. When football scouts tracked him in his junior year, he realized he might be able to earn a football scholarship. Phil had his eye on the University of Tulsa. By now, Phil's father had made a lot of progress in overcoming his addiction to alcohol. Joe decided to start his psychology practice in West Texas and take the family with him. There were very few psychologists in that part of Texas, and Dr. Joe made house calls by airplane. Phil decided to stay in Kansas by himself to finish high school.[21]

Phil never backed down from a fight during his

Phil McGraw's senior portrait from the Shawnee Mission North High School Yearbook.

high school years, and he and his buddies participated in some wild antics outside school. Phil got off work from the Hallmark factory in the wee hours of the morning. He later said he was a "night owl looking for trouble."[22] A friend who worked with Phil owned a Chevy Chevelle muscle car with over four hundred horsepower. After work, the boys raced around the deserted streets at high speeds looking for other cars to drag race.

One deserted night, Phil and three of his friends hurtled down Main Street in downtown Kansas City at over a hundred miles an hour. Suddenly, a patrolman appeared on their tail and ordered Phil's friend to pull over. To Phil, the cop appeared to be a giant as he approached the Chevy and began interrogating the boys. When the cop asked the driver some questions, the boy smart-mouthed the cop. The police officer told him "Buddy, *you just don't get it.*"[23] He then socked Phil's friend so hard he ended up with two black eyes. The next boy to be questioned handled things quite differently. When the

Athletic Scholarship

Colleges and universities offer scholarships for every kind of sport, including baseball, basketball, cross-country, crew, fencing, field hockey, football, golf, lacrosse, soccer, softball, hockey, swimming, tennis, track, and volleyball. Coaches, librarians, and guidance counselors are a good source of information about what is offered and how to apply. Books such as *The Sports Scholarships Insider's Guide* by Dion Wheeler tell the student how to apply for a scholarship at any division. Many websites are devoted to helping the high school athlete find scholarship money—some sites charge a fee for their services.

patrolman questioned him, he answered politely and respectfully. The cop let him alone.

The experience with the patrolman and the two boys taught Phil something about life: some people get it and some people do not. People who do not get it attract pain into their lives. People who get it have a more enjoyable time. Phil decided he would be a person who got it. Eventually, he would teach other people how to "get it" too.[24]

4
LIKE FATHER, LIKE SON

In 1968, Phil McGraw entered the University of Tulsa in Oklahoma on a football scholarship. McGraw arrived at his dorm room wearing sunglasses, carrying his suitcase, his 8-track tape player, and his dress suit. "I am Phil from Kansas City," he told his roommate Ken. After putting his things away and looking around the room, he announced, "I'm taking the top bunk." Ken said okay. He knew right away McGraw was the kind of guy who acted like he owned the place wherever he went.[1]

McGraw's girlfriend Debbie Higgins had also gone away to school. She was studying social work at Southwest Missouri State in Springfield, Missouri. McGraw had given Higgins a promise ring after high school. The two traveled back and forth between Springfield and Tulsa to spend time together.

McGraw played the position of middle linebacker on the freshman football team, but was soon injured on the football field and could no longer play. He left the University of Tulsa at the end of his freshman year. Higgins dropped out of Southwest Missouri State because she could not afford to continue her education at the college.

Deciding to join his family in Texas, McGraw moved to the town of Lubbock. He worked selling memberships in health clubs. Like his father, sales came easily for McGraw, and he soon owned partnership interests in several health clubs.[2]

McGraw asked Higgins to join him in Texas. On May 11, 1970, Debbie moved to Lubbock. On that day a tornado roared through the town, killing 26 people and injuring at least 1,500. Higgins would later say it was a sign of things to come.[3]

Six months later, McGraw and Higgins got married in Debbie's hometown church in Kansas. They honeymooned in Vail, Colorado, then returned to Lubbock to live. After two years in Texas, the young couple moved back to Kansas so Debbie could be closer to her family. Drawing on his knowledge of the health club industry, McGraw opened the Grecian Health Spa in Topeka.

It soon became clear that the young McGraws did not have a happy marriage. One weekend, McGraw flew the two of them from Topeka to Wichita Falls in

his airplane for a family get-together. According to Debbie, not a word was spoken between the two on the four-hour flight. They remained silent with each other during the family visit and on the return trip. Debbie

An aerial view of a residential area in north Lubbock, Texas, on May 11, 1970. The photograph shows the devastation inflicted by a tornado that struck the area earlier that same day.

was unhappy and felt overpowered and stifled in her marriage.[4]

The health and fitness craze was barely off the ground in 1971. Hoping to get in on the ground floor of this promising industry, McGraw, his father, Joe, and two friends from Texas formed a corporation called International Health Resorts, Inc. Phil McGraw was president with 46 percent ownership.[5] In June 1971, International Health Resorts opened the Grecian Health Spa in an exclusive area of Topeka. McGraw had great hopes for the success of the new business.

McGraw and Debbie built a three-bedroom home in a new development on Topeka's west side. McGraw raced around town in his new blue Chevy Corvette convertible. He had also bought a 1965 Mooney airplane that he kept in Wichita Falls.[6] Although Debbie enjoyed their lifestyle, she was not happy. She felt overwhelmed by McGraw's take-charge personality and the fact he wanted her to always look and act in ways that pleased him. When Debbie did not please McGraw in some way, he would freeze her out emotionally and refuse to speak to her. He told her she did not have the mental capacity to carry on a conversation with him.[7]

The Grecian Health Spa did not fulfill McGraw's expectations. The business could not meet payments on its equipment or pay the rent on time. The club closed in September of 1973. A week later the Grecian Health Spa filed for bankruptcy.[8] Phil and Debbie had to sell their home at a loss, and the blue Corvette was repossessed. The McGraws decided to take a separation from their marriage. McGraw returned to his family in Texas, and Debbie stayed with her family in Kansas. McGraw later said they were just too young to be married.[9]

Many people had bought memberships in the

Grecian Health Spa. It was now closed, and the patrons could not get their money back. Complaints poured into the State Attorney General's office about the spa. Vern Miller, the attorney general for the State of Kansas, was cracking down on consumer fraud. His office investigated the Grecian Health Spa but could not find evidence of wrongdoing. No charges were filed against McGraw and his partners.

The McGraws had their brief marriage annulled in a Kansas court. McGraw describes their parting in a lighthearted manner, saying, "We never had a cross word. We just sat down and said, 'Why did we do this?'"[10] Debbie's feelings about the breakup were more bitter. Thirty years later, she told radio disc jockey Randy Miller, "Oh yeah, it was like a death. Then you internalize it and you say, what did I do wrong? . . . it was tough."[11] The two did not see each other again until their thirtieth high school reunion where they had a polite conversation.

In Wichita Falls, Texas, McGraw's life was on hold. His business had failed and so had his marriage. But things were about to change. In the summer of 1973, McGraw met Robin Jameson when she was visiting his sister Brenda. Jameson, a pretty, petite young woman, had graduated from high school the week before. McGraw was immediately attracted by Jameson's spunky personality. Robin saw McGraw as a very kind, nice young man. He asked her out, and they began dating steadily. Although they would continue to date for several years, Jameson knew after six months that McGraw was the man she would marry.[12]

McGraw's father had obtained his license from the Texas State Board of Examiners of Psychologists and was a practicing psychologist. In 1973, Doctor Joe suggested to Phil that he return to college, complete his degree, and join him in a father-son practice. McGraw had long had a keen interest in the human psyche and what made people tick. He decided a degree in psychology would be the way to go. He was especially excited about the idea of a father-son practice and making his dad proud.[13]

The ideal college for McGraw's goals existed in Wichita Falls. Midwestern State University was a small commuter college of about 4,000 students. The campus was attractive, with charming buildings of red brick topped with tile roofs. Best of all, the requirements for entry were not strict. The college accepted almost every student who applied. McGraw, now 25 years old, enrolled in Midwestern as a psychology major.

The psychology department at Midwestern was small, with only about four professors on the faculty. The department's focus was on behavioral psychology. Behavioral psychologists, or behaviorists, believe that humans behave in a way that will pay off for them. Just as rats learn to push the right buttons to get food

Dr. Phil McGraw and his wife Robin at the 30th Annual Daytime
Emmy Awards in 2003.

pellets, so humans seek the right switch to bring about happiness. Situations vary in life, and people can learn what brings pain or happiness in each new situation.[14]

Midwestern's emphasis on results-oriented psychology appealed to McGraw's practical nature. McGraw applied himself to his studies. He completed three years of course work in two years and earned excellent grades. In 1975, McGraw received his bachelor's degree from Midwestern. He continued to take classes, preparing to enter graduate school in psychology.

McGraw chose North Texas State University for his graduate work. North Texas State is about 35 miles north of Dallas, in Denton, Texas. Right away, McGraw stood out from his fellow students. While most grad students drove beat-up old cars, McGraw flew back and forth to the university in his airplane.

While most grad students drove beat-up old cars, McGraw flew back and forth to the university in his airplane.

Outgoing and friendly, McGraw showed an interest in all kinds of people. Former classmate James Cannici said McGraw was nice to everyone, including the janitor and the cleaning lady. "He would take time to talk to them and check in with them in a way most people would not."[15]

The psychology department—located in an old dormitory—included classrooms, psychology clinics, graduate student offices, and the main office. The setup allowed students and professors to mingle on a daily basis. At this time in the mid-seventies, there was quite a debate going on between the behavioral psychologists and the humanist psychologists on the faculty. McGraw agreed with the behaviorists and was not afraid to argue his point of view with his teachers.

McGraw was told he had an "attitude" and would never make it in psychology.[16] But McGraw was inspired by his father's actions to obtain a better quality of life. McGraw wanted to be the second person in his family to finish college. Like his father, he wanted to continue his higher education and earn a Ph.D.[17] He stuck with it and worked hard, asking questions in class and achieving

Behavioral Psychology

Behaviorism was introduced to psychology in 1913 by J. B. Watson. Watson claimed the goal of psychology was to predict and control human behavior. Later, B. F. Skinner studied how rewards and punishments influenced behavior. Watson and Skinner had a major impact on psychology. They believed people who are rewarded for acting in positive ways will continue to act positively. They believed painful consequences can stop negative behavior. Behavior modification has been used to treat drug addiction, alcoholism, and phobias.[18]

Humanist psychology concentrates on exploring human behavior rather than trying to control it. Humanists study the elements of what it means to be human. One of these elements is self-actualization, or a person's potential to fully develop the self. Pioneers in humanism were Abraham Maslow, Carl Rogers, and Rollo May.

excellent grades. In 1976, McGraw succeeded in earning his master's degree.

Shortly thereafter, McGraw married his steady girlfriend of four years, Robin Jameson. Both McGraw and Robin had grown up with alcoholic fathers and avoided drinking. "I probably haven't had a glass of alcohol cumulatively in my whole life," McGraw would later say.[19]

After their wedding, Robin joined McGraw in a modest two-bedroom apartment in Denton while McGraw worked toward his doctor of psychology degree. The young couple were very much in love. According to McGraw, Robin told him "You make the living, and I'll make the living worthwhile."[20] The two were deeply committed to creating a healthy and wholesome life for both themselves and for their future children.

5

BECOMING
DOCTOR MCGRAW

One outstanding professor at North Texas State won McGraw's admiration and friendship. G. Frank Lawlis, Ph.D., was a behaviorist who became McGraw's mentor and doctoral dissertation advisor. Dr. Lawlis specialized in pain management. Lawlis was a pioneer in the field of "mind-body" medicine and believed disease involved more than the physical body of a person. He believed healing involved the mind and spirit as well as the body.[1]

McGraw admired the work Lawlis was doing. He decided to research pain relief for rheumatoid arthritis sufferers for his doctoral dissertation. A dissertation is a report in which the student puts forth a theory in his field of study. The student writes down his research and submits the document to a committee of faculty members. The professors judge the dissertation and decide whether a degree will be granted—in McGraw's case, a doctoral degree in psychology.

McGraw tested 24 women volunteers to see whether relaxation exercises and biofeedback could help them control their arthritis pain. He prepared a questionnaire for them to complete. He included questions about "locus of control" and hoped the women's answers would help him analyze how locus of control affected their pain.

Locus means location, or place. *Control* is mastery or management. According to McGraw, everyone has a locus of control. This locus of control is either inside of a person or outside a person. When locus of control is inside, a person believes she is in control of her life. When it is outside, she believes she is controlled by things that happen outside of her.[2] McGraw believed an inner locus of control was healthier than an outer locus of control. The locus of control theory would become a major teaching tool for McGraw in the future.

McGraw's research was not conclusive. He did not prove that biofeedback and relaxation exercises help patients control their pain. He did not determine with absolute certainty that locus of control was a factor in their pain management. However, psychology is not an exact science. His research was straightforward and thorough. His dissertation was approved and signed by

Dr. Lawlis. Still, McGraw had not yet earned the title of "doctor." To receive that honor, he would have to work as an intern on a psychiatric ward.

McGraw and Robin were adjusting to marriage. Like many newly married couples, they had spats. One night McGraw came home to find Robin sitting in the corner with her arms and legs crossed and a scowl on her face. She refused to speak to him. When he asked what was wrong, she told him "Nothing!" Her words did not match her body language. McGraw felt terrible that she would not be honest with him about her feelings. It took him forty-five minutes of coaxing to get her to open up and admit she was angry before they could work things out. Later, he would use their experience to teach couples to be emotionally honest with each other.[3]

McGraw worked as an intern in the Waco VA Medical Center in Waco, Texas. It was not a pleasant experience for the young grad student. McGraw remembers many of the doctors as petty, power-hungry tormentors. To him, the ward seemed more like a warehouse than a hospital. Many of the patients took Thorazine, a high potency anti-psychotic drug. The stench of "Thorazine-laced urine" was just one more thing he had to endure during long months spent on the ward.[4]

McGraw kept a signed letter of resignation on his clipboard. The letter reminded him he could quit at any time. When one of the doctors behaved in a bizarre or dictatorial way toward him, he could leave. But his goals kept him going. He stayed the course, and in May of 1979 received his Ph.D. He was now Dr. McGraw, just like his father.

McGraw called his father to announce the good news and let him know he was ready to join his dad's practice in Wichita Falls. Excitement filled him at announcing himself as "Doctor McGraw" to his father. Yet McGraw had doubts. He wondered if joining his father's practice would be the best thing for him. Robin waited for him as he made the call. Just for a second, as he met his wife's eyes, he felt she understood his doubts. But they did not talk about it. McGraw had taken a tough journey to become a psychotherapist, and he believed he must now put what he had learned into action.[5]

McGraw did make a promise to himself that day. He vowed that no matter how much money he eventually made, he would not stay with work he did not enjoy. He told himself he would "never sell out and live without passion and fire."[6]

In June 1980, armed with his license to practice psychology, McGraw joined Joe's practice in Wichita Falls. McGraw earned a good living as a therapist. Phil and Robin joined the local country club, where they met many successful people. Wealthy bankers, lawyers, realtors, and their families consulted McGraw in his counseling office.[7]

McGraw preferred salty common sense over theory and could be blunt with clients when they made choices he considered stupid. At the same time, he complimented them for smart choices. Many clients have said they felt safe and protected in his presence and grateful to have him in their corner. Others felt he was not sympathetic enough to their problems.[8] He later said he was a terrible therapist and told *Newsweek* that many of the people who came to see him "just wanted to rent a friend. I'd be sitting there saying, 'You know, here's your problem: you're a jerk.'"[9]

McGraw worked hard and took on extra responsibilities on behalf of his clients. At times, he acted as a negotiator (person who makes deals) for them. One client was going through a divorce. McGraw accompanied her to meetings with accountants. She said having him there took away her fear.[10]

McGraw often served as an expert witness in court cases. McGraw was able to explain complex issues in simple terms so the jury understood the evidence. He became a popular expert witness. He testified in divorce and personal injury cases and in cases involving airplane crashes. He liked the courtroom atmosphere and the no-nonsense way evidence was presented and voted on by the jury.[11]

In 1979, Robin gave birth to their son Jay.

McGraw's joy at the birth of his son soon turned to fear. Three weeks after Jay was born, doctors found the baby had a serious stomach condition. The valve to Baby Jay's stomach had squeezed shut. Surgery was required to keep Jay from starving to death. McGraw felt horror at the prospect of his baby going under anesthesia.

McGraw insisted on carrying Jay to the operating room and staying with his son during surgery. "At that age, it's real easy to go to sleep and not wake up," he later explained.[12] Thankfully, Baby Jay did wake up and recovered completely.

> **McGraw's joy at the birth of his son soon turned to fear.**

When Jay was five years old, McGraw overheard Robin tell a friend that she deeply regretted they could not have any more children. She was sorry she had told McGraw to go ahead and get a vasectomy (an operation that prevents a man from fathering children) after Jay was born. McGraw realized Robin badly wanted another child, and for him to stand in her way was not fair. He decided to surprise his wife and have his vasectomy reversed. He asked a surgeon friend to do microsurgery to reverse the vasectomy. After the operation, he arrived home with baby gifts for Robin to surprise her with his announcement. The reversal was successful, and their second son, Jordan, was born in 1986.

As his sons were growing up, McGraw remembered how distant he felt from his father as a child. He became very involved with his boys.[13] Jay McGraw later talked about the fun games their family enjoyed together. They played one game while watching corny old movies. They turned off the sound and each family member chose a character. As the movie unfolded, they made up lines for their characters. Jay remembers one particular game with his dad: "It came to the big climax where the two gunslingers were getting ready for a gun duel. One stared at the other, and I supplied the line 'So it's come to this, has it?' My dad then spoke up for the other gunslinger, saying 'You just can't take a joke, can you?' I broke up, and he did too."[14]

Things at work were not as joyous as they were at home. McGraw often had arguments with his father. His clients tried his patience with their problems. At times, he felt like clients wanted him to be a

Expert Witness

Lawyers often ask qualified people to explain their areas of excellence in civil and criminal trials. A person who testifies about his specialty is known as an expert witness. The expert witness educates the judge and/or jury about subject matter that pertains to the case. Most witnesses are limited to talking about facts—expert witnesses may also express opinions. For example, in a lawsuit involving a plane crash, an expert in aviation might be called in to testify about the crash. The expert witness could explain the facts of the plane crash as well as expressing his or her personal opinion about why it happened.

"babysitter" instead of a counselor teaching them to take control of their lives.[15] He was often tempted to tell his patients to "get real."[16] Although he had an immensely successful practice, he did not feel excited about his work.[17]

The McGraw family, pictured clockwise from top: Robin, Phil, Jordan, and Jay.

McGraw constantly searched for businesses to become involved in outside his practice. In 1983, McGraw and his father formed a partnership with a former client of Joe's, a businesswoman named Thelma Box. The three launched a personal growth seminar called "Pathways." McGraw's charm and charisma wowed the people who attended the seminars. A big man at six feet four inches and 240 pounds, McGraw was a handsome and imposing person.

After asking the people in his seminars what they wanted, he always asked them two more questions: "What do you have to do to get there?" and "How will you feel when you get there?" The answer to those questions helped people figure out what they really wanted and how to move toward it.[18]

Pathways seminars became so popular, the partners began offering sessions once a month. By the late eighties, hundreds of people were paying $1,000 a piece for McGraw's advice to inspire and direct them in their lives.

In 1987, a complaint was filed against McGraw's father with the Texas State Board of Examiners of Psychologists. The details were never made public because Joe chose to turn in his license in July of 1987. He said he could no longer practice psychotherapy because of his deteriorating health. The Board replied with an Order of Dismissal.

A year later, in 1988, Phil McGraw found himself

in a similar situation. A client filed a complaint against McGraw with the Texas State Board of Examiners of Psychologists. The woman claimed McGraw allowed her family to interfere in their doctor-patient relationship. According to McGraw, the family of the young woman who complained had asked him to "watch out for her," so he had given her a job in his office.

In 1989, McGraw was reprimanded by the State Board and placed under supervision for one year. McGraw later commented on the reprimand, saying, "I kind of file it under the old adage of 'no good deed goes unpunished.'"[19]

McGraw became more and more unhappy with psychology and the Pathways seminars. He thought back to the promise he had made to himself the day he became a doctor: "If I ever find myself doing this just for the money . . . if I am ever just going through the motions, I am out of here."[20]

Finally, he admitted to himself and to Robin that he wanted to quit his psychology practice and take on an entirely different career. Robin supported his decision. The choice, although difficult to make, brought him a huge amount of relief.[21]

6
COURTROOM WIZARD

In 1989, Phil McGraw and his friend Gary Dobbs became partners in a new business. McGraw and Dobbs founded a trial consulting firm they named Courtroom Sciences, Inc. (CSI for short). A trial consulting firm is a company that is hired by law firms to help lawyers prepare for trials. Trial consultants help lawyers select jurors who will be sympathetic to their client's case. They also prepare witnesses and organize evidence to present in the courtroom.

McGraw and Dobbs moved their families 140 miles from Wichita Falls to Dallas, Texas, and opened the firm in the Dallas suburb of Irving. The two men were well-qualified to start such a firm. Attorney Gary Dobbs had served as Director of the State Bar of Texas. McGraw had worked with the airlines creating psychological profiles of pilots after plane crashes and served as an expert witness in many court cases. Dobbs liked McGraw's ability to study people and draw quick conclusions about them.[1] McGraw also had the ability to tell lawyers exactly what was wrong with their case and how to fix it. People said Dobbs had the money while McGraw had the brains, and that was the way they set up the company. Although McGraw and Dobbs were partners, McGraw was the driving force behind CSI.[2]

One thing CSI did to help attorneys was develop a software program called Trial Vision. This software helped lawyers create their own computer presentations to display in court. The software was a big hit with attorneys and made lots of money for McGraw and Dobbs.[3]

McGraw had no regrets about leaving his psychology practice. He found his new career exciting and fulfilling. He compared it to producing and directing a movie. Working behind the scenes, he helped the lawyers prepare their case. Then, he got a front-row seat in the courtroom and watched them put his work into action.[4]

In 1991, McGraw sold his interest in the Pathways self-improvement seminars to devote his entire attention to CSI. His father also sold his interest in Pathways. Joe and Jerry had moved to Irving along with Phil and his family. In 1993, McGraw received the sad news that Joe had heart disease. His dad's health was rapidly failing. McGraw and his father were able to talk out all their differences and express their loved for each other.[5] On August 22, 1993, in the midst of teaching Sunday School, Joe collapsed and died of a heart attack.

Phil's mom had been married to Joe for 53 years. After he died, she did not like living alone in the huge empty house they had shared. Phil and Robin invited Jerry to move into private quarters in their home. The family appreciated Jerry's hard work and loving ways over the years and lavished her with good things. Jay and Jordan were thrilled to have Granma, as they called her, living with them. Jerry lived with them for

McGraw achieved success and fulfillment as Managing Partner of Courtroom Sciences, Inc. in Irving, Texas.

a year before realizing she needed to be independent. She moved into her own small house nearby, where she revived her life-long love of gardening. Working in the garden and on other creative projects made her feel happy.[6]

After his father's death, McGraw spent long hours at CSI. The company became one of the most successful trial consulting firms in the United States, reportedly bringing in $20 million per year. In 1996, Phil, Robin, Jay, and Jordan moved into a five-bedroom mansion on a golf course.

McGraw traveled throughout the United States, Europe, and the Far East for CSI. Clients included Fortune 500 companies, major television networks, and airlines. CSI charged $400 an hour for its services.[7] The company kept a low profile, and McGraw insisted no one at CSI talk to the media. It was crucial that clients trust CSI to keep their information strictly confidential.

McGraw was tough on his employees. He had high standards and expected them to live up to those standards. Employees might be separated from family and friends for weeks and months at a time while traveling with clients. Employees were given a modest salary and earned big bonuses. The harder they worked, the more money they earned. A 60-to-70 hour workweek was not unusual.

If an employee disappointed McGraw, he would

let him know it. One former employee said McGraw would "yell and rant and cuss" when he got angry.[8] Most employees found working at CSI to be exciting and challenging. McGraw could be funny and charming. Biting and witty sayings were a specialty of his. And he was a wizard at predicting how trials would go.

McGraw credits his wife with keeping their marriage alive during the years he was a workaholic. "She chose . . . to focus on my better qualities and the values of our family. She has loved me when I was anything but lovable and stood by me when, but for her, I would have been standing . . . alone."[9]

In 1996, an event happened that was to change McGraw's life forever. At that time, people around the world were terrified of Mad Cow Disease. Thousands of cows were being destroyed in Europe because they had the disease. Horrible images of slaughtered animals appeared every night on the news.

On April 16, 1996, Oprah Winfrey, the queen of daytime television, did a show titled "Dangerous Foods." One of her guests that day was Howard Lyman, Executive Director of the Humane Society's Eating With Conscience Campaign. Lyman was a former cattle rancher turned vegetarian. He talked about Mad Cow Disease and how it spread. Lyman claimed the meat from sick cows was ground up and fed to other cows. Oprah waved her arm through the air in response. She said, "[What you said] has just stopped me cold from eating another burger!"[10]

That day, a Texas cattleman happened to be watching the show. He was furious when he heard Oprah criticizing beef. After the show, the value of beef went down on the stock market. Cattle ranchers blamed Winfrey and called it the "Oprah Crash." The cattleman and a friend filed a lawsuit against Winfrey, her guest Howard Lyman, and her production company, Harpo Productions.

Howard Lyman pets his cat, Caesar, in his Virginia home in 2004. Lyman became a central figure in the court case between Oprah Winfrey and an association of Texas cattle ranchers.

The cattlemen accused Winfrey of ignoring the False Disparagement of Perishable Food Products Act. This act states that no one may criticize perishable food products without scientific proof. The cattlemen sued Winfrey in a lawsuit that could cost her over $100 million if she lost. Extra money was asked for to punish her for the way she was "lambasting the American cattle industry."[11]

Winfrey hired Charles "Chip" Babcock, a Dallas attorney, to defend her. When she learned the trial would be held in Amarillo, Texas, she was frightened.[12] The trial would be right smack in the middle of cattle country. At the airport, a big sign announces to arriving passengers: "Welcome to Cattle Country." Bumper stickers in town announced, "The only mad cow in America is Oprah."

Babcock hired CSI and Phil McGraw to advise their defense team. McGraw advised Winfrey not to focus on whether beef was healthy or unhealthy.

First Amendment

In 1791, The Bill of Rights was added to the United States Constitution to protect the liberties of its citizens. The Bill of Rights includes nine Amendments to the Constitution. The First Amendment protects freedom of the press and freedom of speech. A citizen cannot be punished by the government for stating an opinion in public or in private. The First Amendment also forbids religion established by the government and guarantees a person the right to worship in any religion he chooses. The First Amendment permits citizens to meet together. It also allows citizens to petition the government to right what they consider wrongs.

Instead, he suggested the trial should focus on her First Amendment rights. As an American citizen, Winfrey is allowed by the First Amendment of the United States Constitution to state her opinion without fear of any punishment.

After five weeks of testimony, the jury decided in Winfrey's favor and sent the cattle ranchers home without a penny. Winfrey was thankful to the jurors.

Winfrey believed she owed a lot of credit for her victory to Phil McGraw. She called him one of the smartest men in the world. She invited McGraw, Babcock, and the rest of her defense team to appear on her television show. Later, Winfrey decided McGraw should return to the show by himself. She wanted him to share his "Phil-isms," as she called his wise and witty statements, with her audience.[13]

> **Winfrey believed she owed a lot of credit for her victory to McGraw. She called him one of the smartest men in the world.**

In April of 1998, McGraw made his first solo appearance on *Oprah*. On that show, McGraw listened to a prostitute complain about her terrible life. McGraw told her the first thing she should do is put her clothes on. He told another woman in the audience to get over her self-pity and move forward with her life. Many people did not like McGraw's tough talk. Winfrey's producers advised her to drop him from the show. But Winfrey thought his advice to the prostitute was right on target. She thought it was funny and wise.[14] She believed in McGraw. She decided to invite him back to the show. This time, she would warn her audience that McGraw always tells it like it is.

The second time he appeared, the audience was much more enthusiastic.

7

COUNSELOR AND
LIFE STRATEGIST

McGraw appeared on *Oprah* every Tuesday, and ratings soared with his appearances. Winfrey's audience could not get enough of Dr. Phil's sharp, no-nonsense advice. One of his favorite sayings was "You either get it or you don't." Most of his short, punchy statements focused on the theme of getting it or not getting it.

When McGraw had met with his patients as a psychotherapist, he could not give them his blunt opinions because doing so would have been unprofessional. Now, he was free to combine his honest folksy advice with principles of psychotherapy to advise 20 million viewers every week. He was finally able to "get real" with people who looked to him for guidance.

McGraw referred to himself as a jock. His masculine

looks, direct language, and humorous sayings appealed to men as well as women. As one reviewer put it, "He's a 21-st century cowpoke, genteel enough to talk to the ladies but cowboy enough to punch out the BSers."[1] Everywhere Winfrey went people told her they loved her show and they especially loved Dr. Phil.[2]

Winfrey suggested McGraw write a book. He liked the idea. With the help of a high school English teacher in Irving, Texas, he wrote his first self-help book while continuing to work at CSI and appear on *Oprah*.

The book *Life Strategies: Doing What Works, Doing What Matters* came out in January of 1999 from Hyperion. McGraw dedicated his first book "to my wife, Robin, and her gentle and caring spirit, and to my sons, Jay and Jordan, who inspire me with their vibrancy and energy."[3]

In *Life Strategies*, McGraw introduces his ten "Life Laws." His number one law is: "You Either Get It, or You Don't." According to McGraw, in every situation in life people either get it or they do not. If a person does not "get it," he will end up with a life of frustration and failure. Law Number One is crucial to living a good life and can be learned,

> **McGraw dedicated his first book "to my wife, Robin, and her gentle and caring spirit, and to my sons, Jay and Jordan, who inspire me with their vibrancy and energy."**

McGraw says. Anyone can "get it" if they understand his ten life laws and put them into practice.[4]

Life Strategies soared up the nonfiction bestseller list its first week in print. Winfrey dedicated her entire television show on January 13 to McGraw's book, and McGraw traveled the country talking about *Life Strategies.*

The book was popular with readers, but some critics were not impressed. *Publishers Weekly* said McGraw did a good job of pointing out people's actions that cause failure, but the book had awkward writing and a bullying tone.[5] Readers did not agree. *Life Strategies* quickly hit the *New York Times* bestseller list.

The seventies and eighties spawned many self-help books that portrayed readers as victims of their unhappy childhoods. Some critics referred to the jargon in these books as "psychobabble." McGraw had a low opinion of these books. He called them "largely unfocused, lazy, gimmicky, politically correct, and above all, marketable."[6] In the nineties, readers wanted less "psychobabble" and more old-fashioned straight talk. *Life Strategies* gave them what they wanted. The book sold so quickly that the publisher had to print thousands more copies to keep up with the demand.

McGraw continued to present live seminars for thousands. On *Oprah*, McGraw's appearances often took the form of several shows devoted to solving one problem area, such as marriage, money, or weight loss.

A woman is moved to tears by meeting Dr. Phil at a book signing.

In 2000, McGraw launched a ten-part series on *Oprah* called "The Get Real Challenge." Fifteen thousand people applied for counseling in "The Get Real Challenge." Forty-two were chosen. The group gathered at a hotel for several days of Dr. Phil–style therapy.

McGraw was in complete control of "The Get Real Challenge." He would not answer questions from the participants, telling them he wanted them to learn to answer their own questions. His helpers were dressed in all black and never smiled. The atmosphere was intimidating to some people.[7] Several sessions were filmed and shown on *Oprah*. People in the sessions often had puzzled expressions on their faces, as if they did not quite get what was happening to them. As the week progressed, people seemed more relaxed in their sessions. Many emotional scenes with tears and hugs took place.

After the seminar, several participants appeared on *Oprah* to talk about what they had learned. They said they felt happy and excited about their experiences. They gave Dr. Phil credit for turning their lives

Dr. Phil makes an appearance on the television comedy *Frasier* in 2003.

around. One man said he finally felt free from his past. When McGraw heard their sentiments, he got tears in his eyes. He rarely showed emotion, and Winfrey teased him about his moist eyes.[8]

McGraw became a regular contributor to Winfrey's *O, The Oprah Magazine*, writing a monthly advice column. One column included questions from readers on marital cheating, an abusive co-worker, and a friend who made a stay-at-home mom feel guilty for spending too much time with her children.

In answer to the woman who asked about her abusive co-worker, McGraw addressed the subject of bullying: "The truth is that bullies are found not just at school or on the playground; they also lurk in the workplace." He advised the woman to stop putting up with abusive behavior immediately. He told her to take action before the day ended. He suggested she either confront the woman personally, or if she did not feel comfortable doing that, complain to company management about the abuse.[9]

By December 2000, McGraw had rocketed to celebrity status. He retained literary agent Jan Miller from Dupree/Miller and Associates in Dallas, Texas, to represent him. A literary agent makes deals with publishers and protects authors to make sure they are treated fairly. Miller and McGraw were a good fit, since she represented several famous self-help authors.

McGraw's second book, *Relationship Rescue: A*

The Self-Help Craze

Americans love self-help books and buy them by the millions. Topics covered by self-help authors include how to get rich, how to overcome fear, and how to have better relationships. Library and bookstore shelves are filled with advice on every subject a reader could imagine. Some of today's most popular self-help authors are Wayne W. Dyer (inspiration), Suze Orman (finances), and Dr. Andrew Weil (health).

Seven Step Strategy for Reconnecting with Your Partner, came out in 2000 from Hyperion and gleaned a positive review from *Booklist.* The writer, Nancy Spillman, in a tribute to McGraw's growing celebrity, referred to him as a "high-profile psychologist." She wrote that his "straight-from-the-shoulder enthusiasm and genuine concern shine through the gutsy yet sound advice."[10]

In the Prologue to *Relationship Rescue,* McGraw answers the question that fascinated him as a boy when he wondered what made his grandparents tick and why the Salvation Army boys had slaughtered his football team. Why are some people successful while others are not? He wrote:

> We all know people who get
> all the breaks and opportuni-
> ties, yet who still cannot do
> anything with their lives.
> And we know others who
> seemingly come out of
> nowhere to defy the odds
> and overcome immense

challenges to carve their niche in the world. What I've discovered . . . is that the ones who do well are so in touch with their individual core of consciousness, so aware of their self-worth and their sense of personal value, that they not only treat themselves with enormous self-respect but they inspire others to treat them with equal respect. . . . They have tapped into their core of consciousness, claimed their right to a fulfilling life, and have refused to accept less from themselves or anyone else.[11]

Relationship Rescue, like the book before it, soon topped the bestseller lists.

8
FAMILY
FAME

In June 2001, tragedy struck a close relative of the McGraws. Robin's sister Cindi Broaddus, a divorced mother of three adult daughters, was badly burned when a jar of sulfuric acid crashed through the windshield of her car. The acid had been hurled off a freeway overpass by an unknown assailant.

Robin McGraw kept in constant touch with her older sister during her stay in the Baptist Burn Center miles away from Dallas. She brought soft gowns and comfortable robes and sat for hours by her bedside. But it was Phil McGraw who made Broaddus laugh: "My brother-in-law has always had that effect on me, even in this condition [when] I didn't know I was capable of laughter."[1] The McGraws kept in close touch with Broaddus and helped her financially as her rehabilitation was progressing.

McGraw was appearing regularly on *Oprah*, and questions poured into the show from teenagers about the problems in their lives. McGraw decided to write a book for young people. His son, Jay, at the time a 21-year-old college student, had a better idea. Jay told his dad he thought he should be the one to write the book. Jay believed teens could relate better to a young guy. McGraw and his publisher liked the idea.

Life Strategies for Teens by Jay McGraw was published in December 2000 by Fireside, the paperback division of Simon & Schuster. The book, aimed at kids 12 and older, was a younger version of Phil McGraw's book *Life Strategies*. Jay's book focused on the Ten Life Laws and included exercises for kids to put the laws into action. Both McGraws now had books on the *New York Times* bestseller list.

In the fall of 2001, McGraw was named one of *People*'s sexiest men of the year. A picture of McGraw and his dog appeared in the magazine under the headline: "Sexiest Self-Help Guru." Jay noticed his dad had become a sex symbol when the two stayed at a hotel where the boy band 'N Sync was staying. He said the mothers of the band's fans recognized McGraw and swarmed him asking for pictures and autographs.[2]

Several months after Jay's book *Life Strategies for Teens* was published, Simon & Schuster announced it had signed Dr. Phil McGraw to a multimillion-dollar deal for four books. At the same time, the giant publisher signed Jay to three more books.

Jay's second book, *Closing the Gap: A Strategy for Bringing Parents and Teens Together*, came out in 2001. Jay, like his dad, honors family members on the book's dedication page. Along with his parents and brother Jordan, he dedicates *Closing the Gap* to his

Jay McGraw poses in his Dallas apartment on September 10, 2001. His second book, *Closing the Gap: A Strategy for Reconnecting Parents and Teens*, was released in November that year.

grandmother: "And to my grandma Jerry, who doesn't hear often enough how much I love her. Grandma is just plain awesome!"[3]

Closing the Gap had short, punchy chapter titles such as "The Wake-Up Call," "Teen Myths," "Parent Myths," "Parent Poisons," and "Teenage Land Mines." The book's format was designed to appeal to young people, with bold graphics, purple accent color, and cartoon-like illustrations.

One myth Jay McGraw debunked in *Closing the Gap* was that teens have no power. In an interview with Diane Sawyer, he said, "We have a lot of influence in the decisions that our parents make just by the way we act around them."[4] *Closing the Gap* soared onto the bestseller lists.

In the fall of 2001, tragedy struck the country. On September 11, terrorists attacked the United States killing nearly three thousand Americans. The entire country went into shock and mourning. McGraw decided to devote a live seminar to helping people cope with tragedy.

To show how people can undergo trauma and survive, McGraw invited his sister-in-law Cindi Broaddus onstage to share her story of trauma and recovery. She told the audience how an unknown attacker had hurled acid off a freeway overpass into her car, burning her beyond recognition. She shared how her family was there for her during the long weeks and months of

Dr. Phil throws the ceremonial first ball before a game between
the Washington Nationals and Atlanta Braves in Washington on
September 20, 2006.

recovery. When she finished speaking, the audience of thousands cheered for her. McGraw then surprised her with a new White Chevy Trailblazer.

Broaddus later wrote about the event in her book *A Random Act*: "I'd always said I'd do anything for Phil. I think his work is that important. . . . Phil baptized me, albeit by fire, into the world of sharing my story with thousands of people and witnessing the lights in their hearts glow for a stranger. He also helped show me that terrible events don't have to have terrible outcomes."[5]

Phil McGraw's third book, *Self Matters*, hit bookstores on November 13, 2001, and it spent over 40 weeks on the bestseller charts. The book filled the number one slot for 13 weeks. *Self Matters* sold 1.3 million copies in 2002 and was ranked the best-selling nonfiction book of 2002 by *Publishers Weekly*.

In *Self Matters*, McGraw wrote that the way for people to be truly happy is to learn who they are and find their passion in life. By figuring out the "ten defining moments," "seven critical choices," and "five pivotal people" in their lives, readers would understand how they had gotten to their present place in life. Once they understood how they had gotten into their situation, they could take steps to correct it. [6]

McGraw shares personal stories in *Self Matters* as he does in all his books. He writes that when he finally decided to leave his career as a psychologist, "I immediately felt vibrant and alive, as though I had gained back those ten years. My life energy surged without limit."[7]

McGraw has said many times there is nothing new under the sun and his books are basically common sense. The critics agreed. "When you get past the showmanship, Dr. Phil is preaching an ancient message: Know thyself," wrote Marcia Z. Nelson of *The Christian Century* in her review of *Self Matters*.[8]

"Readers familiar with McGraw's aggressive TV personality may be surprised by this book's thoughtful and serious tone . . ." *Publisher's Weekly* opined. "His book offers a thorough, realistic resource for those who are committed to turning their lives around to get what they really want and need."[9]

McGraw appeared on the most popular television talk shows of the day, including *Larry King Live*, *Dateline* with Jane Pauley, and *Good Morning America* with Diane Sawyer. Barbara Walters chose him as one of the "Ten Most Fascinating People" for her 2002 television special. Ratings soared as audiences tuned in to hear McGraw's take on life.

McGraw appeared on the cover of the September 16, 2002, issue of *Newsweek*. The article inspired pro and con opinions from readers on Dr. Phil's methods. Murray Shaw, 93, wrote to say that he agreed with McGraw on how to live a successful life: "Let him know that there is someone with a little life experience

Dr. Phil's popularity began to soar even as some of his methods and views were criticized by mainstream psychologists.

who thinks as he does." A therapist urged care in telling folks to get real. "To attempt to engage in sound-bite therapy is dangerous," warned letter-writer Susan J. Elliott.[10]

Warnings were ignored. People could not wait to sign up for "get real" moments with Dr. Phil. Thousands attended his live seminars. He achieved phenomenal success as a life strategist, garnered high ratings on *Oprah*, and spent weeks on the bestseller lists. He even wrote workbooks to accompany all his bestselling books. It seemed as if there were only one place left for Dr. Phil to go from that point—television.

> **People could not wait to sign up for "get real" moments with Dr. Phil.**

Oprah Winfrey had believed McGraw should have his own daytime talk show. McGraw liked the idea on the condition that he could be himself. He would not do fashion shows or makeovers and he would not have celebrities on his show unless they were willing to "get real." Agreeing that McGraw would be in complete control of the show, Winfrey's production company, Harpo, teamed up with Paramount to produce the *Dr. Phil* show.

In December of 2002, the McGraws moved from Dallas, Texas, to the Westside of Los Angeles, California. They rented a home for several months before buying a mansion in Beverly Hills costing a reported $7.5 million dollars. The mansion had five bedrooms, a guesthouse, a three-car garage, and a pool area lined with palm trees. Robin decorated the interior with sculptures of dancing women, jewel-studded crosses, crystal chandeliers, and dozens of lush pillows.[11] McGraw drove a $200,000 Ferrari around Southern California. The McGraws also purchased a luxury condominium in the Turtle Creek area of Dallas, where they could stay when visiting family or handling business concerns in Texas.

In Los Angeles, Paramount hired a production staff to brainstorm topics and investigate possible guests for the *Dr. Phil* show. The process of preparing to launch the show took just under two years. According to journalists Sophia Dembling and Lisa Gutierrez, the production staff was not happy with McGraw. One person who quit the show told the

Ten Life Laws From *Life Strategies* by Dr. Phillip C. McGraw:

One—Get Real

Two—You Either Get It, or You Don't

Three—You Create Your Own Experience

Four—People Do What Works

Five—You Can't Change What You Don't Acknowledge

Six—Life Rewards Action

Seven—There Is No Reality; Only Perception

Eight—Life Is Managed; It Is Not Cured

Nine—We Teach People How To Treat Us

Ten—There Is Power In Forgiveness

journalists that McGraw was overbearing to the staff. The former employee said that in 25 years of being in television production, he had never felt such negative vibes on a show.[12]

It was reported in *Us Weekly* that the television staff considered walking out because of poor working conditions. They complained about the close quarters and long hours. *Us* reported that staff members were expected to work around the clock. They would bring changes of clothing and sleep on chairs pulled together.[13]

McGraw replied calmly to the criticism: "Am I hard on people? Have I raised the bar of expectancy? . . . Yes . . . [and I] make no apology for it whatsoever. None whatsoever. We do have high expectancies here."[14]

Oprah Winfrey made a trip to the studio to encourage everyone who worked on the show. Her visit had a soothing effect, and the staff continued to work hard. Despite the staff's complaints, they predicted *Dr. Phil* would be an amazing show.[15]

9
TELEVISION
GURU

*D*r. *Phil* **premiered** on September 16, 2002, with a show called "Families Under Stress." Not since *Oprah* debuted in 1986 had a syndicated television show pulled in such high ratings.

On his first show, McGraw counseled several families by giving them doses of his blunt advice. He delivered his favorite question with a twang and a smile: "What were you *thinking*?" McGraw's first guest was a single mom he scolded for yelling at her kids. Without Oprah's warm, accepting personality as a contrast, critics wondered if McGraw's television popularity would last.

But McGraw was not about to soften his style. He had warned entertainment executives well in advance that he would do the show his way: "If I can deliver scientifically sound, responsibly presented information to

[Americans] in the privacy of their own homes, for free, on a regular basis, that is a good thing." McGraw added that he takes his job "very, very seriously. I have a very spontaneous delivery style, but . . . I've done an awful lot of homework and come in what I think is really prepared."[1]

Viewers liked Dr. Phil's style. Millions tuned in to his show every day.

The *Hollywood Reporter* called *Dr. Phil* "entertainment with a little self-help thrown in." The critic wrote that although Dr. Phil claimed his show was not voyeurism (taking pleasure in observing other people's problems and tragedies), she believed "there is nothing more voyeuristic than watching a guest getting chewed out by Dr. Phil in front of millions." She added that McGraw's likable personality and obvious sense of calling would propel the *Dr. Phil* show to success.[2]

The hour-long *Dr. Phil* show is the same format Monday through Friday. The show is filmed on a set of shining dark wood accented with electric blue. A live audience of mostly women waits with anticipation for McGraw to appear onstage. McGraw strolls onstage to a booming musical introduction. He walks down several steps and saunters around the stage, waving to the audience. The audience cheers.

Every *Dr. Phil* show deals with a problem, such as obesity. The guests who appear that day all struggle with that particular problem. Staffers prepare 50–60

In addition to helping everyday people, celebrities (such as actress Lindsay Lohan, above) are also interviewed by Dr. Phil on his television show.

page notebooks on each guest so McGraw will know all the details about them before he interviews them. Before the show airs, guests are filmed in their homes dealing with the problem on a daily basis. Those scenes are played on the show.

McGraw's guests sit in chairs facing him and the audience while he questions them and analyzes their choices. He mentions a few things they have done right. Then, he lectures them on what they may have done wrong. McGraw does not speak like a psychologist. He uses down-home phrases such as "That dog won't hunt!" and "How's that workin' for ya?" The entertaining and humorous sayings can jolt guests into looking at their problems in a new way.

In the final moments of the show, McGraw advises guests how to solve their problems and live happier lives. Often, he will have an expert add to his advice. Dr. G. Frank Lawlis is a clinical psychologist who appears on the show. Lawlis was McGraw's mentor at North Texas State University. Lawlis often advises the guests to get additional counseling or check into a rehabilitation hospital to get off drugs or alcohol or deal with out-of-control anger. McGraw calls this "aftercare," and all of Dr. Phil's guests are entitled to it. "The show is the beginning, not the end," McGraw says. "I've been a therapist. I know what it takes for people to make lasting and meaningful change. I am not attempting to substitute a twelve-minute conversation with me for six months or a year or three years of therapy."[3]

At the end of the show, McGraw waves goodbye as he strolls into the audience. He heads straight for his wife Robin and takes her hand. They smile and chat as they walk offstage together. McGraw has received criticism for hurrying his petite wife off camera. He says it is the other way around. "When I'm by myself I generally kinda walk like I lost something," he says. "She walks like a speed demon."[4]

Why would people want to appear on *Dr. Phil* and share their most intimate problems with millions of television viewers? Dan Neil, writing for *Los Angeles Times Magazine*, reflected on the question: "Apart from

Dr. Phil and his wife, Robin, join several other celebrity guests in singing along with the president and first lady during the annual Christmas in Washington concert on December 12, 2004.

the bewitching prospect of appearing on 211 [television] stations nationwide . . . guests . . . receive a lot of free counseling and expensive rehabilitation . . ." Neil goes on to say that although he has his doubts about the show, "I think [McGraw's] counseling is astute and direct and commendably free of jargon . . . I appreciate that he sticks up for children and tells parents whining about their needs to stop being such awful, selfish monsters."[5]

Critic Michelle Cottle agreed: "Truth be told, some folks don't need to learn to love themselves so much as they need to stop being such [idiots]. On some level, the joy of watching Dr. Phil is that he does what most of us would love to do: speak truth to idiocy."[6]

On the other hand, many psychology professionals have criticized *Dr. Phil.* An article in *Psychology Today* said, "Many psychotherapists concede that Dr. Phil is a brilliant diagnostician who immediately isolates his subjects' problems—but caution that this very skill can be dangerous. Psychotherapy isn't about the practitioner finding the right answer, but about guiding the patient to an answer and helping him deal with it appropriately."[7]

McGraw's qualifications have been called into question. Peter M. Barach, a psychiatry instructor at Case Western Reserve University, wondered whether McGraw was staying within the limits of his ability, adding "the guy hasn't had a real practice in 15 years."[8]

McGraw does not claim to be doing therapy. He is one of what *Psychology Today* refers to as the new 21st century advice-givers. McGraw calls himself a "life strategist" who uses his thirty years of experience in the field of psychology to help people live happier lives. When asked whether he considered the television show therapy or entertainment, he said he considered it education. Although we learn reading, math, and facts about the Civil War in school, McGraw believes our educations are not complete. We do not learn much about how human beings function or how to make relationships work. "Very few people in America ever go to therapy," he says. "If they don't go to therapy or get a book and read it where else are they going to get it?"[9]

People Magazine compared McGraw's counseling to a trusted mechanic probing underneath the hood of a car. "He lets the engine run, listens for the problem, then gets in there with a wrench."[10] There is one area where McGraw does not allow any loose bolts: drug and alcohol abuse. "Deal breakers!" he says. "Absolute, drop-dead, zero-tolerance deal break-ers . . . drugs and alcohol are substances that, if abused, create an altered state of consciousness. When you are dealing with a drug- or alcohol-controlled partner, you are dealing with the drug or the alcohol, not with the partner."[11]

McGraw makes no apology for being judgmental in this area. "I know that I am being intolerant here—but I intend to be. . . . You must be prepared to leave your rela-tionship until such a time when your partner can objectively verify to you

The Alcoholic Family

Alcoholics are unpre-dictable people. In order to cope with the alcoholic's behavior, alcoholic families tend to live by rigid rules. Children learn that talking about their feelings and trying new things are not allowed. Family problems are not discussed outside the family. Children of alcoholics often deny their feelings about what they see happening in the family. They may have trouble knowing what is real and what is not real. Fear, anger, and hurt often haunt these children. It is hard for them to grow into mature men and women. Many seek treat-ment in therapy to help them become healthy, functioning adults.[14]

that the problem is under control and that he or she is in a program of ongoing monitoring and treatment."[12]

McGraw, himself, experienced the pain of alcoholism growing up with a drunk and raging father. His wife also grew up in an alcoholic family. McGraw does not drink alcohol. Many of his television shows are devoted to substance abuse problems. Rehabilitation and counseling are often provided by the *Dr. Phil* show for men, women, and children who are hooked on drugs or alcohol. McGraw estimated that at least twenty episodes of his show's third season were devoted to substance abuse.[13]

> **McGraw estimated that at least 20 episodes of his show's third season were devoted to substance abuse.**

Americans enjoyed watching McGraw relate to the people on his show. He did not take any nonsense and was not shy about telling them where he stood. Most interactions with guests include humorous moments. *Dr. Phil* continues to soar in popularity and keep its place right below *Oprah* at the summit of daytime television.

10
GIVING
BACK

The boy who once ate ketchup-and-mustard sandwiches for dinner had become Dr. Phil, a self-help sensation known around the world. McGraw's books had sold more than 10 million copies and been published in 30 different languages. People rushed to buy Dr. Phil merchandise such as workbooks, calendars, CDs, T-shirts, caps, and mugs. McGraw was now a brand name, and his income increased along with his success.

In 2003, McGraw's fourth book, *The Ultimate Weight Solution: The 7 Keys to Weight Loss Freedom*, appeared in bookstores and resulted in the usual phenomenal sales. McGraw dedicated the book "To all of those people who are sick to death of riding the 'diet roller coaster' in pursuit of the elusive goal of a fit and trim life.'"[1] McGraw thanked Oprah Winfrey for "coming up with such a great title for the book" and for her friendship, kindness, and support.[2]

Robert H. Eckel, M.D., Chair of the Council on Nutrition, Physical Activity, and Metabolism for the American Heart Association endorsed the book: "Dr. Phil has cut through the confusion of fad diets with clinically supported sound information and action plans for lasting weight management," he wrote.[3]

McGraw understands the sadness of obesity. He shared with readers that obesity had gravely affected many members of his family. He said he had worked with many obese patients and promised readers that in his book they would find a lasting way to slim down.[4] Jay's book on weight control for teens would follow close behind his father's.

McGraw wanted to share his wealth with those in need, especially children. One of the things that mattered most to him was helping children who were grossly overweight and who suffer from diabetes.[5]

McGraw wanted to share his wealth with those in need, especially children.

On October 22, 2003, McGraw announced the formation of the Dr. Phil Foundation, a nonprofit organization focusing on fighting childhood obesity. McGraw stated that childhood obesity affected twice as many children as it did in the previous generation. "As a regular contributor to many charities," McGraw announced to the press, "I am excited to create the Dr. Phil Foundation specifically dedicated to a cause that I am passionate about on a personal and professional level—the obesity crisis in America."[6]

The foundation would be pursuing contributions from a variety of sources. McGraw would pay 100 percent of the administrative costs for the foundation. That way all monies could go directly to selected organizations to help them.[7]

The first person McGraw asked to serve as a trustee on the board of the new foundation was Robin's sister Cindi Broaddus. Broaddus felt a new sense of purpose in her life after the criminal attack that had scarred her and was thrilled at his invitation. She told McGraw she would be honored to serve as a trustee with other trusted colleagues of McGraw's.[8]

In September 2004, McGraw's fifth book, *Family First: Your Step-by-Step Plan for Creating a Phenomenal Family*, hit bookstores and was an immediate bestseller. In chapter one, McGraw reveals his feelings of isolation and agony growing up in a family beset by alcoholism and poverty.[9]

In *Family First*, McGraw's goal is to help families find balance and harmony in their lives. To demonstrate how his advice could help families in turmoil, McGraw invited troubled families to appear on the

Dr. Phil show. The families volunteered to spend several weeks in counseling with McGraw. In one such family, the wife and mother had been married three times and had five children by four different men. The last child, up for adoption, was the product of an affair with a co-worker. Through all of this, the husband had stayed with her. This behavior caused critics to compare *Dr. Phil* to crass talk shows with obnoxious guests who behaved in outrageous ways to get higher ratings. *Dr. Phil's* ratings did indeed go up when these families appeared on the show.[10]

McGraw says turmoil in families can be avoided when the family has a plan. *Family First* tells parents how to create such a plan by setting goals for their families. In the book, McGraw advises parents how to avoid the mistakes his own family made. One thing parents should do, according to McGraw, is catch their kids doing something right. "Far too often, kids hear about what they've done wrong." He advises parents to start praising their children for positive behavior and tell them they're doing a great job.[11]

Dr. Robert H. Schuller interviewed McGraw and asked why he wrote *Family First*. "I wrote *Family First* as a celebration of family and a call to arms for parents," McGraw said, "because I truly believe that families in America are under attack. I just believe that family is being eroded by so many forces that we have to get our eye on the ball and put family back in America."[12]

McGraw told Schuller that parents are not meant to be friends to their kids. It is not their responsibility to buy kids every toy and article of clothing they want. He said a parent's main job is to be a leader and a provider for their children, spiritually and physically.[13]

Although McGraw gives his own parents credit for what they did right, such as teaching him a good work ethic, he is honest about what they did wrong. He says he grew up in a dysfunctional family. A dysfunctional family is one that does not act in healthy ways. Dysfunctional families keep secrets about things like alcohol abuse and mental illness among family members. They often ignore problems, so the problems never get solved and may continue in future generations. McGraw tells the truth about his family even when it is not pretty. In *Family First*, he urges parents to make a plan to overcome dysfunction and create strong, healthy families.

> **A dysfunctional family is one that does not act in healthy ways.**

McGraw dealt with the recurring theme of substance abuse again in May of 2005 when he appeared on *Larry King Live* to talk about his television special with Pat O'Brien. O'Brien was a well-known television broadcaster who had just been released from a rehabilitation hospital for drug and alcoholic addiction. O'Brien was now clean and sober and in recovery.

King asked McGraw why O'Brien left vulgar telephone messages on a woman's voicemail. McGraw replied that when a person is using drugs or alcohol, the substances take over the person's mind and can cause them to act in ways they would not act when sober. "[Drugs and alcohol] potentate one another," he told King. In other words, they make each other more powerful. "That's what happens with the dangerous combination with the interactive effects between drugs and alcohol."[14]

On a different topic, King asked McGraw about a tabloid story that questioned his friendship with Oprah Winfrey. McGraw said he and Winfrey were wonderful, lifelong friends. He joked that the only problem he had with Oprah is that she and his wife Robin went shopping together too often. "She's a dear friend and always will be," he said.[15] Winfrey and McGraw have maintained their business partnership as well as their friendship. Winfrey's production company, Harpo, continues to co-produce the *Dr. Phil* show.

In December 2005 McGraw's sixth book, *Love Smart: Find the One You Want—Fix the One You Got* came out from Free Press, a division of Simon & Schuster, and soared up the bestseller lists. Paula Chin, writing in *Ladies Home Journal*, called the book a

In 2005, Dr. Phil did a television special with Pat O'Brien (above) that dealt with recovery from drug and alcohol addiction.

"no-nonsense guide to finding the right person, creating a true connection and sustaining love and respect over the long, difficult road that is marriage."[16]

In an appearance at the Crystal Cathedral in Garden Grove, California, McGraw told the Reverend Robert Anthony Schuller that too many people are "loving dumb." McGraw said they have reversed the natural order of friendship, dating, and marriage. Too many people begin a relationship with sex, he said, thus their friendship is not allowed to build and deepen. McGraw believes that the 50 percent divorce rate in the United States stems directly from "loving dumb."

To love smart, McGraw suggests each person start with self. "If you wouldn't date you, why would anybody else date you? You got to fall in love with yourself, you got to decide, you know, God made me very uniquely, specifically to be the way I am. . . . Don't try to be something you're not. Don't try to be some media image of some anorexic person barely standing there. You got to be who you are."

People looking for a mate often put high importance on looks. McGraw says it is not about looks, it is about beliefs. "What we are after is someone that will create in you the experience of peace; the experience of belongingness, the experience of being meaningfully connected and it truly is all about values."[17]

Reverend Robert Anthony Schuller referred to McGraw as "a man of inspiration and faith." McGraw responded that the McGraws have a God-centered home.[18] McGraw is committed to his Christian faith. He believes that each person's relationship with God is personal. He believes God has a plan for each and every person, and everyone is gifted with specific gifts and talents.[19]

In January 2006 McGraw teamed up with the Internet dating service Match.com in a partnership that would teach a broader audience of single people how to "love smart."

McGraw believes the best partners complete each other. He is glad Robin has qualities different from his: "I want to be married to somebody who has the qualities and characteristics that are not primary within me so that that person can bring things to the table that help complete me. What's

Children and Obesity in America

"Obesity in America has reached epidemic proportions," says E. Chester Ridgeway, M.D., Past–President of The Endocrine Society. The Surgeon General of the United States reports that overweight in adolescents has tripled over the past two decades. Young people now experience diseases once seen only in adults—including cardiovascular disease, hypertension and type 2 diabetes. Obesity can cause youngsters to have low self-esteem and feel uncomfortable in social situations. Dr. Ridgeway remains hopeful, saying, "together, we can take small steps to beat the condition with a balanced combination of behavior change, medical/scientific understanding, and intervention."[20]

more, I promise you my wife does not want to be married to someone exactly like her."[21]

Robin McGraw has acquired her own reputation as a gifted and talented celebrity. Fans love seeing her on the show and write asking for her advice. Her first book, *Inside My Heart: Choosing to Live with Passion and Purpose*, was published by Thomas Nelson and appeared in bookstores in September 2006.

11
FAMILY
FIRST

The *Dr. Phil* **show** continued to attract a huge daily audience. Viewers wrote asking for names of therapists trained in McGraw's methods. McGraw recruited his longtime friend and mentor, Dr. G. Frank Lawlis, to train licensed professionals in the Dr. Phil methods of counseling.

The *Dr. Lawlis Series on Dr. Phil's Approaches* trains licensed therapists, psychologists, social workers, and professional coaches in the Dr. Phil approach to therapy. Students may take two courses, pass the required test, and receive an associate therapist certificate. A senior therapist certificate will be issued to those who take four courses and pass the required test. Courses are offered online.

Once a student has been trained by Dr. Lawlis and

receives a certificate, he or she is eligible to provide counseling using McGraw's methods.[1]

McGraw's concern for the welfare of American children led him to expand the charitable giving of the Dr. Phil Foundation. On January 20, 2006, McGraw and his wife Robin announced a personal donation to the Dr. Phil Foundation of $1 million from the McGraw family. The donation officially kicked off "Dr. Phil's Million Dollar Challenge for the Children." The challenge invites donations for children in foster care, and children in need nationwide. The McGraw family has promised to cover all administrative costs so that every dollar donated will be used directly to support children.[2]

The goal of McGraw's foundation is to help foster children like Luz. Luz appeared on the *Dr. Phil* show to tell her story. After moving to the United States from Mexico, Luz and her seven siblings lived in a garage with their parents. "My father was very violent with everyone. . . . We were beaten a lot," she told McGraw's audience. Luz's father murdered her two-year-old sister and five-year-old brother and forced his family to help him bury the bodies. He was eventually sentenced to the death penalty. Luz's mother was sent to prison and later deported.

At the age of eleven, Luz got a lawyer and contacted the press. "I moved a lot of people and they actually let me stay with the kids," she reported. Luz's brothers and sisters managed to remain in the same household in their six years in foster care.

Luz has overcome many obstacles and continues to work hard and excel in school. The Dr. Phil Foundation arranged for Luz to receive a full four-year scholarship to the University of San Diego, a 2004 Hyundai Accent, one thousand dollars in free gas from Shell Oil Company, and free cell phones so she and her brothers and sisters can stay connected while she is at school.[3] As Chairman of the Board of the Dr. Phil Foundation, McGraw continues to provide critically needed services to young people.

When Hurricane Katrina hit the Gulf Coast on August 29, 2005, the storm devastated the city of New Orleans and caused terrible suffering among the people of the Gulf Coast region. In response, McGraw visited Dallas, Houston, and New Orleans to personally express hope and support to survivors, rescuers, and evacuees. *Dr. Phil* devoted several shows to victims of Katrina. Families were brought to Los Angeles and provided with financial support and housing. Episodes of *Dr. Phil* showed McGraw presenting housing to the families who were staying at the Dream Center, a church in Los Angeles. The families expressed gratitude at having their own private places to live.

Audiences continued to tune in to *Dr. Phil* by the millions. McGraw's latest contract guarantees television shows through the year 2014.[4] McGraw also

Partially submerged homes and vehicles along a residential street in New Orleans in the aftermath of Hurricane Katrina on September 14, 2005.

qualifies as among the top echelon of public speakers, along with such celebrities as Bill Clinton and Colin Powell, earning $100,000-plus for a speaking engagement.[5]

In April 2006, in a spirit of fun, and because he loves scary movies, McGraw made a cameo appearance in *Scary Movie IV*, a parody of the horror movie *Saw*. In the opening scene, McGraw and famous basketball player Shaquille O'Neill are chained together in a bathroom and must use their wits to escape before a deadly nerve gas kills them.

At home, McGraw is just a regular guy. He claims all his days are pretty much the same. He gets up, goes to his office, does what he has to do, goes to the tennis court and runs around for a couple of hours, goes home, and gets into his favorite old green lounge chair that Robin gave him many years ago. He has said, "I don't feel like a celebrity because I don't feel like celebrities look, if you know what I mean."[6] He is an avid athlete who loves tennis, golf, and scuba diving.

Admired around the world for his savvy advice, McGraw has heroes of his own, and most of them are

A stray dog roams a New Orleans street after the floodwaters from Hurricane Katrina have receded. Dr. Phil aided the recovery effort in New Orleans by helping individual families and also publicizing the disaster on his show.

Shaquille O'Neal and Dr. Phil in a scene from *Scary Movie 4* (2006).

in his own family. He honors Robin as his source of strength and the heart of the family. He often says his wife deserves the credit for their successful marriage of over thirty years. He compliments his sons, Jay and Jordan, for their energy and humor. He honors his parents—mother Jerry for her love and sacrifice for her family, and his father Joe for never giving up and continuing to grow spiritually over the years.

One of McGraw's most valued heroes is a woman who would not be considered that special by most people. Robin's sister Cindi Broaddus, scarred by acid thrown at her by an unknown assailant, is a valued member of McGraw's inner circle. McGraw has called Broaddus "one of the biggest heroes in my life" for the way she put aside bitterness and rose above her pain and disfigurement to help others.[7] Her story eventually resulted in legislation making it a criminal act to throw an object from an overpass.

McGraw says his family is his base of operations and his strength in life. Through the years, his love for his wife and sons has been his guiding light. "My family lifts me up and loves me without condition," he writes. "If a man's worth is reflected in the life and spirit of his wife and family, I am truly a wealthy and blessed man."[8] For Dr. Phil McGraw, family truly does come first.

Charities in America

Giving to charities has always been a big part of American culture. Institutions such as the YMCA, American Red Cross, and Salvation Army top the list of favorite charities in the United States. Charities receive 80 percent of their money from individual givers. When a person makes a donation to a charity, it is tax deductible. In most states, a division of the State Attorney General's office regulates charities to make sure they use donations in an ethical and appropriate way.

CHRONOLOGY

1950   Born on September 1 in Vinita, Oklahoma.

1952   Father quits job as high school football coach and goes to work for the oil industry. Family moves throughout Southwest.

1958   Meets pilot Gene Knight and decides to get his pilot's license.

1962   Flies airplanes under his father's supervision.

1964   Moves with his father, Joe, to Kansas City while Joe completes his internship in psychology.

1968   Graduates from Shawnee Mission North High School in Overland Park, Kansas.

1968–1969 Attends University of Tulsa on a football scholarship.

1969   Injured on football field and drops out of the university.

1970   Marries high school sweetheart Debbie Higgins.

1971   Opens the Grecian Health Spa in Topeka, Kansas, where he and wife Debbie live.

Grecian Health Spa files for bankruptcy.   **1973**
McGraw's marriage to Debbie annulled.
He returns to Texas.

Attends Midwestern State University in   **1973–1975**
Wichita Falls, Texas. Graduates with B.A. in
Psychology. Begins graduate studies at North
Texas State University.

Receives master's degree from North Texas State **1976**
University. Marries second wife Robin.

Awarded a Ph.D. in clinical psychology from   **1979**
North Texas State University. Joins father Joe's
psychology practice in Wichita Falls, Texas.

First son Jay is born.   **1979**

Holds first personal growth seminar.   **1983**

Second son Jordan is born.   **1986**

Disciplined by the Texas Board of Examiners of **1988**
Psychologists. Leaves Wichita Falls for Dallas.

Partners with attorney Gary Dobbs to found   **1990**
Courtroom Sciences, Inc. (CSI).

Father Joe dies of heart attack while teaching   **1993**
Sunday School.

1996	Oprah Winfrey is sued by Texas cattlemen. Winfrey's lawyer hires McGraw and CSI to assist with her defense.
1998	Winfrey's six-week trial ends with jury finding in favor of Winfrey. McGraw appears on her show with her legal team. Begins appearing on *Oprah* as a regular guest.
1999	First book, *Life Strategies*, is published by Hyperion. *Life Strategies* becomes bestseller as do all McGraw's books.
2000	Jay McGraw's first book, *Life Strategies for Teens*, is published. Phil McGraw's second book, *Relationship Rescue*, is published.
2001	McGraw's third book, *Self Matters*, spends thirteen weeks at number one on the bestseller lists. Jay's second book, *Closing the Gap: A Strategy for Bringing Parents and Teens Together*, is published.
2002	The *Dr. Phil* show debuts with the highest ratings for a talk show since Oprah Winfrey's debut in 1986.
2003	*The Ultimate Weight Solution: The 7 Keys to Weight Loss Freedom* is published. Jay's book, *Ultimate Weight Solution for Teens: The 7 Keys to Weight Freedom*, is published. McGraw

launches The Dr. Phil Foundation with a
focus on curing childhood obesity.

Family First: Your Step-by-Step Plan for   **2004**
Creating a Phenomenal Family is published.

Love Smart: Find the One You Want—Fix the   **2005**
One You Got is published. McGraw travels to
the Gulf Coast to counsel those affected by
Hurricane Katrina. McGraw announces expanded
giving of The Dr. Phil Foundation for children's
charities with a personal donation of $1 million
from the McGraw family.

CHAPTER NOTES

Chapter 1. Midnight Meeting

1. Sophia Dembling and Lisa Gutierrez, *The Making of Dr. Phil: The Straight-Talking True Story of Everyone's Favorite Therapist* (Hoboken: John Wiley & Sons, 2004), p. 121.

2. Phillip C. McGraw, *Life Strategies* (New York: Hyperion, 1999), p. 2.

3. Mark Peyser, "Paging Dr. Phil," *Newsweek*, September 2, 2002, p. 50.

4. McGraw, p. 3.

5. Ibid., p. 4.

6. Ibid., p. 6.

7. Ibid.

8. Dembling and Gutierrez, p. 122.

9. McGraw, p. 8.

10. Skip Hollandsworth, "Profile of Phillip McGraw," *Texas Monthly*, September 1999, p. 142.

Chapter 2. Country Boy

1. Sophia Dembling and Lisa Gutierrez, *The Making of Dr. Phil: The Straight-Talking True Story of Everyone's Favorite Therapist* (Hoboken: John Wiley & Sons, 2004), p. 1.

2. Ibid., p. 1.

3. Ibid.

4. Laura Yorke, "Self Help: How Dr. Phil Fixed Himself," *Reader's Digest*, April 2005, p. 156.

5. Dembling and Gutierrez, p. 5.

6. Ibid.

7. Phillip C. McGraw, *Life Strategies* (New York: Hyperion, 1999), p. 20.

8. Vinita Chamber of Commerce, <http://www.Vinita.com/events/climate-events.htm> (March 30, 2006).

9. Dembling and Gutierrez, p. 9.

10. "Dr. Phil Getting Real," *Biography*, A & E Television Networks, 2002.

11. Dembling and Gutierrez, p. 4.

12. Ibid.

13. Ibid., pp. 4–5.

14. Phillip C. McGraw, *Self Matters: Creating Your Life from the Inside Out* (New York: Simon & Schuster, 2001), p. 36.

15. Ibid., p. 37.

16. "Dr. Phil Getting Real."

17. Federal Aviation Administration, n.d., <http://www.faa.gov/pilots/become/faq/> (March 22, 2006).

18. McGraw, *Self Matters*, pp. 99–101, 119.

Chapter 3. Taking Flight

1. "Dr. Phil Getting Real," *Biography*, A & E Television Networks, 2002.

2. Phillip C. McGraw, *Family First: Your Step-by-Step Plan for Creating a Phenomenal Family* (New York: Simon & Schuster, 2004), p. 5.

3. Sophia Dembling and Lisa Gutierrez, *The Making of Dr. Phil: The Straight-Talking True Story of Everyone's Favorite Therapist* (Hoboken: John Wiley & Sons, 2004), pp. 18–19.

4. McGraw, p. 6.

5. Ibid., p. 4.

6. Dembling and Gutierrez, p. 21.

7. McGraw, p. 4.

8. Ibid., p. 66.

9. Lily Bosch, "Dr. Phil: Your Total Life Makeover," *Good Housekeeping*, March 2004, p. 120.

10. McGraw, p. 65.

11. Dembling and Gutierrez, p. 11.

12. Phillip C. McGraw, *Self Matters: Creating Your Life from the Inside Out* (New York: Simon & Schuster, 2001), p. 17.

13. Ibid., p. 238.

14. Dembling and Gutierrez, p. 21.

15. "Dr. Phil Getting Real."

16. McGraw, *Self Matters*, pp. 266–267.

17. Dembling and Gutierrez, p. 27.

18. Phillip C. McGraw, *Life Strategies*, (New York: Hyperion, 1999) pp. 20–21.

19. "Dr. Phil Getting Real."

20. Dembling and Gutierrez, p. 38.

21. Ibid., p. 36.

22. McGraw, *Life Strategies*, p. 28.

23. Ibid., p. 29.

24. Ibid., pp. 29–30.

Chapter 4. Like Father, Like Son

1. "Dr. Phil Getting Real," *Biography*, A & E Television Networks, 2002.

2. Sophia Dembling and Lisa Gutierrez, *The Making of Dr. Phil: The Straight-Talking True Story of Everyone's Favorite Therapist* (Hoboken: John Wiley & Sons, 2004), p. 45.

3. Ibid., p. 46.

4. Ibid., pp. 47–48.

5. Ibid., p. 54.

6. Ibid., p. 63.

7. Ibid., p. 47.

8. Ibid., pp. 56–57.

9. "Dr. Phil Getting Real."

10. Mark Peyser, "Paging Doctor Phil," *Newsweek*, September 2, 2002, p. 50.

11. Dembling and Gutierrez, p. 50.

12. "Dr. Phil Getting Real."

13. Phillip C. McGraw, *Self Matters*, (New York: Hyperion, 1999), p. 2.

14. John A. Mills, *Control: A History of Behavioral Psychology* (New York: New York University Press, 1998), p. 4.

15. Peyser, p. 50.

16. Dembling and Gutierrez, p. 72.

17. McGraw, p. 2.

18. Mills, p. 1.

19. "Dr. Phil Getting Real."

20. Kate Coyne, "Dr. Phil: Change Your Life . . . for Good!," *Good Housekeeping*, November 2005, p. 142.

Chapter 5. Becoming Doctor McGraw

1. G. Frank Lawliss, *Transpersonal Medicine* (Boston: Shambhala, May 2001), p. 8.

2. Phillip C. McGraw, *Self Matters: Creating Your Life from the Inside Out* (New York: Simon & Schuster, 2001), p. 168.

3. Phillip C. McGraw, *Relationship Rescue: A Seven-Step Strategy for Reconnecting with Your Partner* (New York: Hyperion, 2000), pp. 130–131.

4. McGraw, *Self Matters*, pp. 1–2.

5. Ibid., p. 3.

6. Ibid.

7. Sophia Dembling and Lisa Gutierrez, *The Making of Dr. Phil: The Straight-Talking True Story of Everyone's Favorite Therapist* (Hoboken: John Wiley & Sons, 2004), pp. 81–82.

8. "Dr. Phil Getting Real," *Biography*, A & E Television Networks, 2002.

9. Mark Peyser, "Paging Doctor Phil," *Newsweek*, September 2, 2002, p. 50.

10. Dembling and Gutierrez, p. 85.

11. Ibid., pp. 95–96.

12. "Dr. Phil Getting Real."

13. Greg Adkins, et al., interview with Jay McGraw, *People Weekly*, November 22, 2004, p. 26.

14. Jay McGraw, *Closing the Gap: A Strategy for Reconnecting Parents and Teens* (New York: Simon & Schuster, 2001), p. 190.

15. Dembling and Gutierrez, pp. 82–83.

16. Arlene Weintraub, "Getting Real—And Getting Real Rich," *Business Week*, June 21, 2004, p. 109.

17. McGraw, *Self Matters*, p. 4.

18. Dawn Raffel, "Oprah's Secret: How to Get What You Really Want," *Redbook*, February 1999, p. 106.

19. "Dr. Phil Getting Real."

20. McGraw, *Self Matters*, p. 4.

21. Ibid., p. 9.

Chapter 6. Courtroom Wizard

1. "Dr. Phil Getting Real," *Biography*, A & E Television Networks, 2002.

2. Sophia Dembling and Lisa Gutierrez, *The Making of Dr. Phil: The Straight-Talking True Story of Everyone's Favorite Therapist* (Hoboken: John Wiley & Sons, 2004), pp. 96–97, 99.

3. Ibid., p. 98.

4. Ibid., p. 99.

5. "Dr. Phil Getting Real."

6. Phillip C. McGraw, *Self Matters: Creating Your Life from the Inside Out* (New York: Simon & Schuster, 2001), pp. 82–83.

7. Dembling and Gutierrez, p. 104.

8. Ibid., p. 110.

9. Phillip C. McGraw, *Relationship Rescue: A Seven-Step Strategy for Reconnecting with Your Partner* (New York: Hyperion, 2000), p. 297.

10. *The Oprah Winfrey Show*, "Oprah's Report on Mad Cow Disease," Show Transcript, April 15, 1996, p. 2.

11. Dembling and Gutierrez, pp. 115–116.

12. "Dr. Phil Getting Real."

13. Ibid.

14. Ibid.

Chapter 7. Counselor and Life Strategist

1. Marcia Z. Nelson, "Getting Real with Dr. Phil," *The Christian Century*, September 25, 2002, p. 23.

2. "Dr. Phil Getting Real," *Biography*, A & E Television Networks, 2002.

3. Phillip C. McGraw, *Life Strategies* (New York: Hyperion, 1999), Dedication.

4. Ibid., p. 30.

5. Jonathan Bing, Jeff Zaleski, Paul Gediman, Review of *Life Strategies: Doing What Works, Doing What Matters, Publisher's Weekly*, December 14, 1998, p. 67.

6. Ana Marie Cox, "I'm OK, You Suck," *Reason*, May 2002, p. 53.

7. Sophia Dembling and Lisa Gutierrez, *The Making of Dr. Phil: The Straight-Talking True Story of Everyone's Favorite Therapist* (Hoboken: John Wiley & Sons, 2004), p. 127.

8. Ibid.

9. Phillip C. McGraw, "Advice, Etc.," *O Magazine*, February 2006, p. 61.

10. Nancy Spillman, Review of *The [sic] Relationship Rescue: A Seven Step Strategy for Reconnecting with Your Partner, Booklist*, November 1, 2000, p. 559.

11. Phillip C. McGraw, *Relationship Rescue: A Seven-Step Strategy for Reconnecting with Your Partner* (New York: Hyperion, 2000), p. 3.

Chapter 8. Family Fame

1. Cindi Broaddus with Kimberly Lohman Suiters, *A Random Act: An Inspiring True Story of Fighting to Survive and Choosing to Forgive* (New York: William Morrow, 2005), p. 64.

2. "Dr. Phil Getting Real," *Biography*, A & E Television Networks, 2002.

3. Jay McGraw, *Closing the Gap: A Strategy for Reconnecting Parents and Teens* (New York: Simon & Schuster, 2001), Dedication.

4. "Dr. Phil Getting Real."

5. Broaddus, p. 141.

6. Phillip C. McGraw, *Self Matters: Creating Your Life from the Inside Out* (New York: Simon & Schuster, 2001), p. 25.

7. Ibid., p. 308.

8. Marcia Z. Nelson, "Getting Real with Dr. Phil," *The Christian Century*, September 25, 2002, p. 23.

9. Excerpt from *Publisher's Weekly* review of *Self Matters*, Amazon Web site, n.d., <http://www. amazon. com/gp/product/>.

10. Mark Peyser, "Paging Doctor Phil," *Newsweek*, September 2, 2002, p. 50.

11. Kate Coyne, "Dr. Phil: Change Your Life . . . for Good!," *Good Housekeeping*, November 2005, p. 140.

12. Sophia Dembling and Lisa Gutierrez, *The Making of Dr. Phil: The Straight-Talking True Story of Everyone's Favorite Therapist* (Hoboken: John Wiley & Sons, 2004), pp. 146–147.

13. Michael Lewittes, "They've had their Phil," *Us Weekly*, October 7, 2002, p. 6.

14. Dembling and Gutierrez, p. 148.

15. Lewittes, p. 6.

Chapter 9. Television Guru

1. Karen Peterson, "Dr. Phil Dishes Advice Right in Your Face," *USA Today*, October 14, 2002.

2. Marilyn Moss, "Dr. Phil," *Hollywood Reporter*, September 18, 2002, p. 11.

3. Peterson.

4. Gregory, p. EO1.

5. Dan Neil, "Training Wheels for the Brain," *Los Angeles Times Magazine*, September 11, 2005, p. 5.

6. Michelle Cottle, "Daddy Knows—The Bad Doctor," *The New Republic*, December 27, 2004, p. 19.

7. Pamela Paul, "Dear Reader, Get a Life," *Psychology Today*, July/August, 2003, p. 56.

8. Gregory, p. EO1.

9. Jeffrey Ressner, "10 Questions for Dr. Phil," *Time*, September 13, 2004, p. 8.

10. Anonymous, Cover Story, *People*, December 30, 2002, p. 102.

11. Phillip C. McGraw, *Relationship Rescue: A Seven-Step Strategy for Reconnecting with Your Partner* (New York: Hyperion, 2000), p. 280.

12. Wayne Kritsberg, *The Adult Children of Alcoholics Syndrome* (New York: Bantam, 1988).

13. Anonymous, Cover Story, *People*, December 30, 2002, p. 102.

14. Mark Glassman, "Synergy for Viacom: Dr. Phil of CBS Interviews Pat O'Brien of CBS," *New York Times*, May 2, 2005, p. C–1.

Chapter 10. Giving Back

1. Phillip C. McGraw, *The Ultimate Weight Solution: The 7 Keys to Weight Loss Freedom* (New York: Simon & Schuster, 2003), dedication.

2. Ibid., ix–x.

3. Ibid., p. 15.

4. Ibid., pp. 22–23.

5. Cindi Broaddus with Kimberly Lohman Suiters, *A Random Act: An Inspiring True Story of Fighting to Survive and Choosing to Forgive* (New York: William Morrow, 2005), p. 196.

6. Dr. Phil Foundation Web site, n.d., <http://www.drphilfoundation.org/>.

7. Ibid.

8. Broaddus, p. 196.

9. Phillip C. McGraw, *Family First: Your Step-by-Step Plan for Creating a Phenomenal Family* (New York: Simon & Schuster, 2004), pp. 3–6.

10. Paige Albiniak, "Phil's New 'Family,'" *Broadcasting & Cable*, February 9, 2004, p. 25.

11. Phillip C. McGraw, "Dr. Phil's Five Ways to Build a Phenomenal Family," *Redbook*, October 2004, p. 134.

12. Robert H. Schuller, interview with Dr. Phil McGraw, *The Saturday Evening Post*, March/April 2005, p. 56.

13. Ibid.

14. Larry King, interview With Dr. Phil McGraw, *CNN Larry King Live*, May 2, 2005, CNN transcript, p. 11, <http://transcripts.cnn.com/TRANSCRIPTS/0505/02/lkl.01.html> (November 25, 2005).

15. Ibid., p. 10.

16. Paula Chin, "Real (Not Sugar-Coated) Secrets to a Happy Marriage," *Ladies Home Journal,* January 2006, p. 94.

17. Robert Anthony Schuller, interview with Dr. Phil McGraw, January 8, 2006, *Hour of Power,* transcript, <http://www.hourofpower.org/interviews/_detail.cfm?ArticleID=4137>, pp. 2–3.

18. Ibid., p. 3.

19. Phillip C. McGraw, *Relationship Rescue: A Seven-Step Strategy for Reconnecting with Your Partner* (New York: Hyperion, 2000), p. 289.

20. Obesity in America Web site, n.d., <http://www.obesityinamerica.org/obesitybasics.html>.

21. Ibid., p. 263.

Chapter 11. Family First

1. Training in Dr. Phil's Methodology Web site <http://www. learndrphilfromlawlis.com/main/index.cfm>.

2. Dr. Phil McGraw's Official Web site <http://www.drphil.com/>.

3. Dr. Phil Foundation Web site <http://www.drphilfoundation.org/>.

4. Kate Coyne, "Dr. Phil Change Your Life . . . for Good!," *Good Housekeeping,* November 2005, p. 142.

5. Michael Learmonth, cover story, *Variety,* October 18–October 24, 2004, p. 1.

6. Sophia Dembling and Lisa Gutierrez, *The Making of Dr. Phil: The Straight-Talking True Story of Everyone's Favorite Therapist* (Hoboken: John Wiley & Sons, 2004), p. 228.

7. Cindi Broaddus with Kimberly Lohman Suiters, *A Random Act: An Inspiring True Story of Fighting to Survive and Choosing to Forgive* (New York: William Morrow, 2005), pp. xi, 151.

8. Phillip C. McGraw, *Relationship Rescue: A Seven-Step Strategy for Reconnecting with Your Partner* (New York: Hyperion, 2000), Acknowledgments.

BOOKS BY DR. PHIL McGRAW

Life Strategies, 1999

The Life Strategies Workbook, 2000

Relationship Rescue, 2000

The Relationship Rescue Workbook, 2000

Self Matters, 2001

The Self Matters Companion, 2002

The Ultimate Weight Solution, 2003

The Ultimate Weight Solution Cookbook, 2004

Family First, 2004

The Ultimate Weight Solution Food Guide, 2005

The Family First Workbook, 2005

Love Smart, 2005

FURTHER READING

Broaddus, Cindi with Kimberly Lohman Suiters. *A Random Act: An Inspiring True Story of Fighting to Survive and Choosing to Forgive*. New York: William Morrow, 2005.

Kritsberg, Wayne. *The Adult Children of Alcoholics Syndrome*. New York: Bantam Books, 1988.

Lawlis, G. Frank. *Transpersonal Medicine*. Boston: Shambhala, 2001.

McGraw, Jay. *Life Strategies for Teens*. New York: Simon & Schuster, 2000.

McGraw, Jay. *Closing the Gap: A Strategy for Reconnecting Parents and Teens*. New York: Simon & Schuster, 2001.

INTERNET ADDRESSES

Dr. Phil McGraw's Official Website
http://www.drphil.com/

Dr. Phil Foundation
http://www.drphilfoundation.org/

Training in Dr. Phil's Methodology
http://www.learndrphilfromlawlis.com/main/index.cfm

INDEX

A

addiction, alcohol and drug, 23–25, 30, 42, 87-88, 94

aftercare, 84, 88

Amarillo, Texas, 7, 8, 59

A Random Act, 75

athletic Scholarships, 31

B

Babcock, Charles (Chip), 10, 59, 60

bullying, 20, 67

Broaddus, Cindi (Sister-in-Law), 70, 73, 75, 91, 105

Bush, President George W. and First Lady Laura, 85

C

charities in America, 105

Clinton, Bill, 102

Closing the Gap, 72–73

Courtroom Sciences, Inc. (CSI), 53-57, 59, 63

critics, 64, 68, 76, 78, 82, 84–87

D

Dobbs, Gary (CSI partner), 53

Dream Center, Los Angeles, 101

The Dr. Lawlis Series on Dr. Phil's Approaches, 99–100

The Dr. Phil Foundation, 90–91, 100

Dr. Phil Show, 78–84, 92, 94, 99–101

dysfunctional family, 93

E

expert witness (definition), 49

F

False Disparagement of Perishable Food Products Act, 59

Family First, 91-93

First Amendment, 59–60

foster children, 100–101

G

"The Get Real Challenge," 65–66

"Getting it," 31–32, 62–64

GI Bill, 16

Grecian Health Spa, 36–37

H

Harpo Productions, 58, 78, 94

Higgins, Debbie (First wife), 10, 59-60

Hurricane Katrina, 101, 102, 103

I

Inside My Heart by Robin McGraw, 98

K

King, Larry, 76, 93–94

Knight, Gene, 19

L

Lawlis, Dr. G. Frank, 43, 45, 84, 99

lawsuit (definition), 11
Life Strategies, 63–64
Life Strategies for Teens, 71
locus of control, 44
Lohan, Lindsay, 83
Love Smart, 94
Lyman, Howard, 57, 58

M
Mad Cow Disease, 8, 57
Match.com, 97
McGraw, Brenda (Sister), 18, 23, 37
McGraw, Deana (Sister), 14, 18, 23, 26
McGraw, Donna (Sister), 14, 18, 23
McGraw, Jay, 47–49, 56, 71, 72, 104
McGraw, Jerry (Mother), 13–16, 26, 54-55, 73, 104
McGraw, Joe (Father), 13–17, 24–28, 35–36, 46, 49, 51, 54–56, 88, 104
McGraw, Jordan, 48, 56, 72, 104, 65
McGraw, Phil (Dr. Phillip C.), 15, 24, 28, 30, 39, 50, 55, 65, 66, 77, 83, 85, 104
    as airplane pilot, 19, 22, 40
    as athlete, 20, 24, 26, 29–30, 33-34, 103
    as courtroom consultant, 7–12, 54, 56, 59-60
    as health club entrepreneur, 34–36
    birth of son Jay, 47–48
    birth of son Jordan, 48

birthplace, 13–14, 17
childhood and family life, 13–32
childhood homes, 14, 20, 27–29
Christian faith, 97
death of father, Joe, 55
defining moment, 21
doctoral dissertation, 43–45
education, 28-30, 33, 38, 40–41, 43–44
expert witness, 47, 49
hi-jinks, 31
marriage annulment to Debbie Higgins, 37
marriage to Debbie Higgins, 34
marriage to Robin Jameson, 42, 45
mentors, 19, 25, 43, 45, 84, 99
motorcycle, 27-28
Ph.D., 46
poverty, 24, 26, 29
relationship with father, 22–25, 27–28, 35, 38, 41, 46, 49, 51, 54–55, 104
relationship with sons, 49
Sexiest Self-Help Guru (*People Magazine*), 71
valley of death, 25, 26
McGraw, Robin Jameson (Wife), 37, 39, 42, 45–47, 56–57, 63, 65, 70, 79, 84, 85, 94, 97–98, 100, 104

Miller, Jan, 67
mind-body medicine, 43–44

N
’N Sync, 71

O
obesity, 90–91, 97
O’Brien, Pat, 93, 94, 95
O’Neill, Shaquille, 102, 104
The Oprah Winfrey Show,
    60–67, 71, 78, 80, 90, 94
O, The Oprah Magazine, 67

P
Pathways Seminars, 51–52,
    54
“Phil-isms,” 60
pilot’s License, 20
psychology, Behavioral and
    Humanistic, 41

R
Relationship Rescue, 68–69

S
Sawyer, Diane, 73, 76
Scary Movie IV, 102

Schuller, Reverend Robert
    Anthony, 96
Schuller, Reverend Robert H.,
    92–93
self-help, 64, 67, 68
Self Matters, 75–76
September 11, 2001, 73
Stevens, Mabel and Cal
    (maternal grandparents),
    18–19

T
Ten Life Laws, 63–64, 71, 79
Texas State Board of
    Examiners of Psychologists,
    51–52

U
The Ultimate Weight Solution,
    89–90

V
Vinita, Oklahoma (birth-
    place), 13–14, 17

W
Winfrey, Oprah, 7–12, 10,
    57–61, 63, 67, 78, 80, 90,
    94

ABOUT THE AUTHOR

Mary Main is the author of mystery novels and biographies for young people and teaches creative writing to children and adults. She enjoys writing about family and friends, and her personal essays often appear in her local newspaper. Her previous biography for Enslow is titled *Isabel Allende: Award-Winning Latin American Author*.

DR. PHILLIP C. MCGRAW

One of the most visible and recognizable men in America today, Dr. Phillip C. McGraw is a best-selling author, life coach, and the star of *The Dr. Phil Show*.

Dr. Phil was not always wealthy and successful. As a boy growing up in the Southwest, he was plagued by family instability and poverty. His experiences as a child and young adult taught him that setting firm goals and working hard would eventually result in the life he wanted. He still uses these principles to guide people today. Dr. Phil's combination of psychotherapy, folksy humor, and common sense advice continue to make him one of America's most popular celebrities.

Mary Main has created a portrait as forthright as the man himself and will give readers fresh insight into the phenomenon that is Dr. Phil.